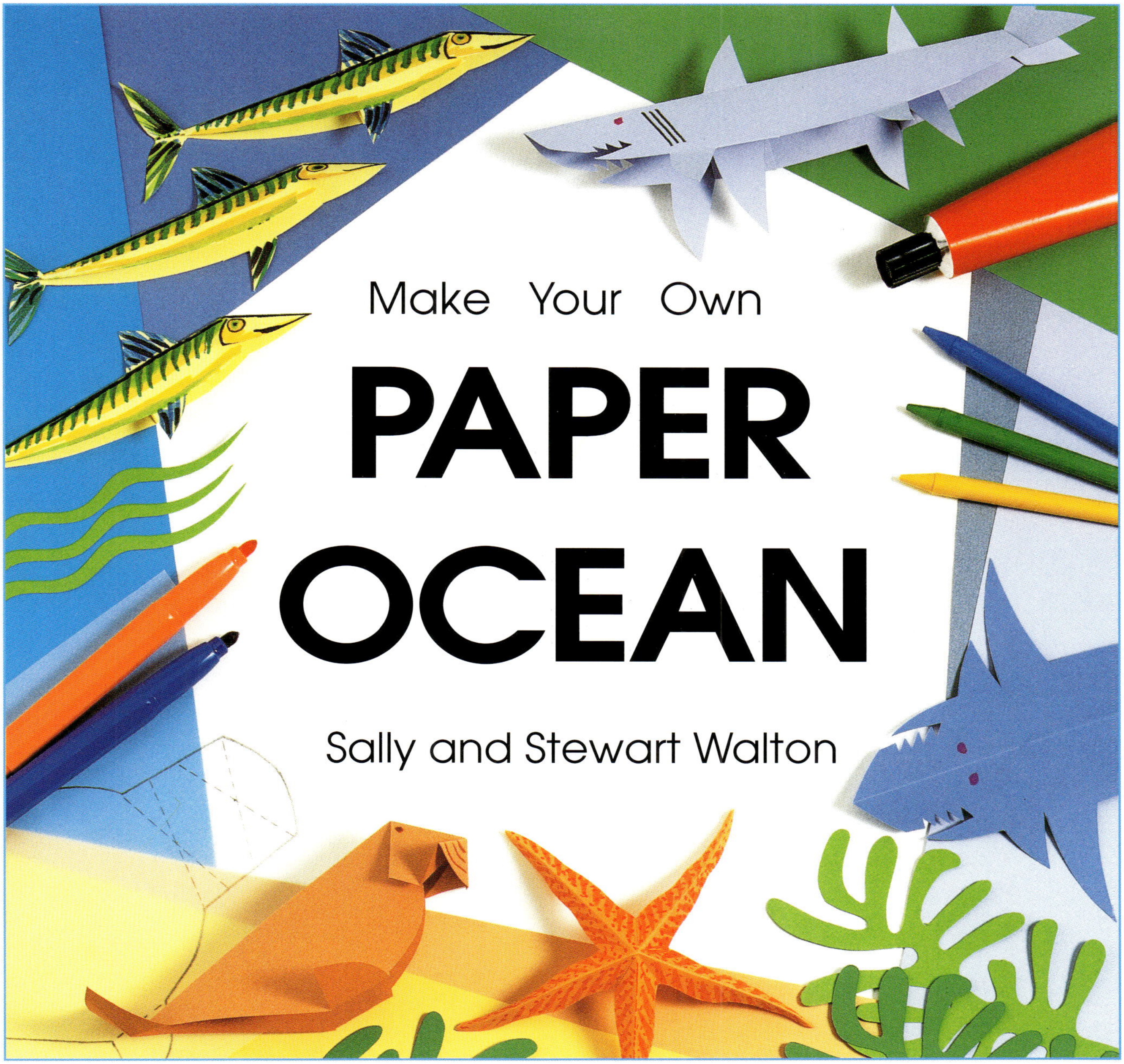

Make Your Own

# PAPER OCEAN

Sally and Stewart Walton

SMITHMARK

This edition published in 1994 by
SMITHMARK Publishers Inc.,
16 East 32nd Street,
New York, NY 10016.

1 2 3 4 5 6 7 8 9

SMITHMARK books are available for bulk purchase for sale promotion and premium use. For details write or call the manager of special sales, SMITHMARK Publishers Inc.,
16 East 32nd Street, New York,
NY 10016; (212) 532-6600.

**ISBN 0-8317-5967-4**

Printed in Belgium.

*For Ruby*

## CREDITS

**Editor:** Helen Stone
**Designer:** Jane Molineaux
**Additional design by:** Rachael Stone
**Photographer:** Jonathon Pollock
**Stylist:** Cherry Randell
**Diorama artist:** John Mac
**Crafts inspector:** Leslie Thompson
**Color separation by:** Scantrans Pte. Ltd., Singapore
**Printed in Belgium by:**
Proost International Book Production

# Contents



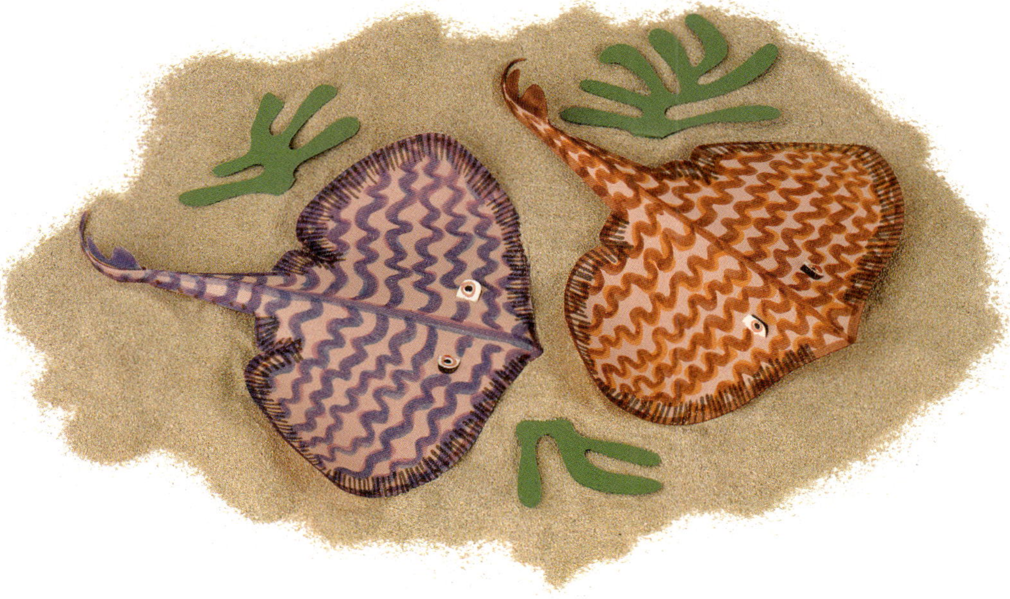

# Introduction

Create your own underwater scene, complete with fish, turtles, sharks, and dolphins, using just a few sheets of stiff paper and some basic equipment.

Each of the projects in this book features facts about the sea creature and has a full-size pattern for you to trace and transfer onto colored paper. Step-by-step instructions explain how to fold your paper patterns into wonderful 3-D models, which you can then decorate.

When you have made the animals, why not make some scenery to place them in using the patterns on pages 18 and 23? Then open out these pages to reveal a colorful ocean diorama, which is the perfect setting for your models.

**Materials** – Each project has a list of materials you will need. Construction paper or thick cartridge paper work best and can be bought from art or craft supply stores. Thin paper makes floppy models and some thick paper is too difficult to cut and fold.

**Safety Tips** – Be very careful with scissors. When you are not using them, lay them in a safe place with the blades closed. You may wish to use small, pointed scissors for some of the smaller cuts; nail scissors are best, but make sure an adult knows you are using them. One or two of the projects in this book may require the use of a craft knife; always ask an adult to make these cuts for you.

**Getting Started** – Before you begin any project in this book, read through the steps here to learn the basic techniques.

### 1. Tracing Patterns

Lay tracing paper onto the animal pattern and hold it firmly in place. Using a soft, sharp pencil, carefully trace the solid outline first and then trace all the fold lines. Take time to get the tracing right. Place your tracing face down onto colored paper. Hold the two together with paper clips and firmly redraw over the traced lines to transfer the pencil outlines onto the paper.

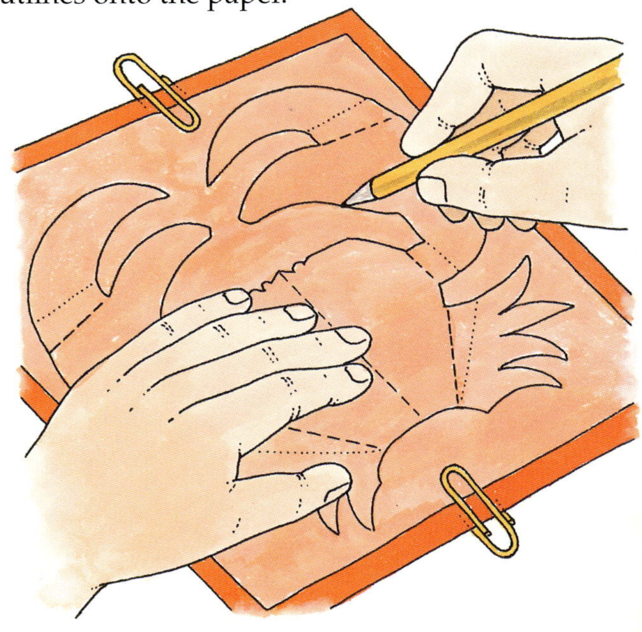

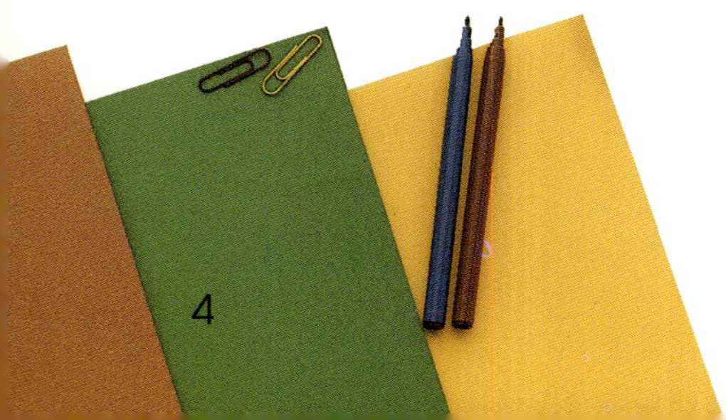

## 2. Cutting Out the Main Shapes

On each pattern, the solid lines are the ones you should cut around and the broken lines are the ones you should fold. Cut out the main shape first and then cut around details such as mouths, gills, and fins. Use round-ended scissors where possible and ask an adult to help you if you find some of the smaller cuts difficult.

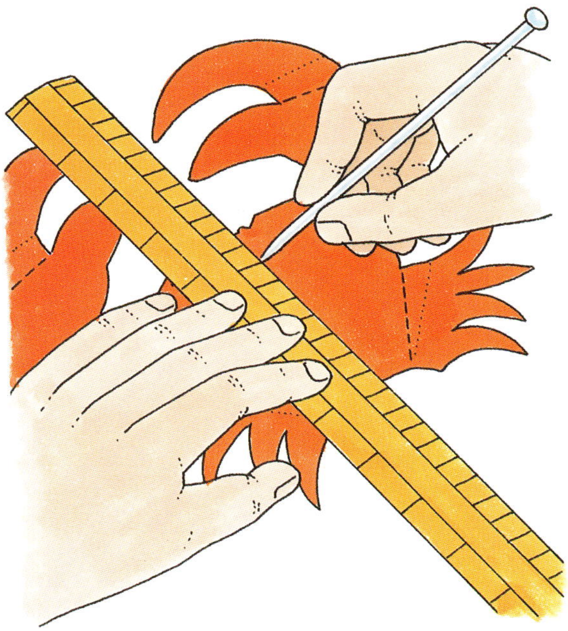

## 3. Creasing the Fold Lines

Before folding the paper, you should crease all the broken lines to make the folds neat. Lay a ruler along the fold line and lift the paper up against it. Hold it in this position, taking care that the ruler does not slip. Run your finger along the bottom edge where the paper lifts against the ruler. Alternatively, keep the paper flat and draw over the fold line with a knitting needle or a ballpoint pen that no longer works, using a ruler as a guide. Don't press too hard – you only want to dent the paper.

## 4. Making Folds

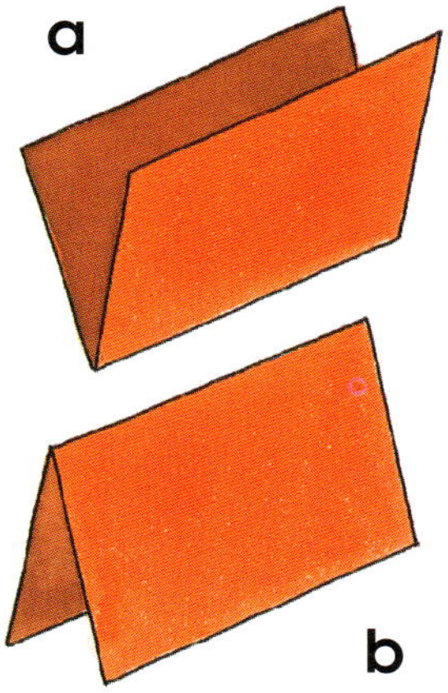


There are two types of folds: valley folds, which dip downward (*a*) or mountain folds, which pop upward (*b*). All downward folds are marked on the pattern by dotted lines and all upward folds are marked by dashes. If you have creased the folds accurately, folding your models will be quick and easy.

## 5. Decorating Your Model

If you are copying the decorations from the patterns in this book, it is easiest to unfold your model and lay it flat. Colored markers, pencil crayons, or crayons work best. Paint may make the paper buckle. If you are making up your own decorations, you may find it easier to color onto the folded model. Make the patterns as realistic or as wild as you like and for the best results, erase any pencil lines before you begin.

## 6. Using the Diorama

Pages 19 to 22 contain a fun scene for you to open out and place your finished models in front of. Stand your book upright on a flat surface and fold out the pages of scenery patterns so that they are at right angles with the rest of the book. You may want to use paper clips to keep them in position. Place your paper scenery in front of the diorama and you have a wonderful ocean scene for your paper fish to swim in.

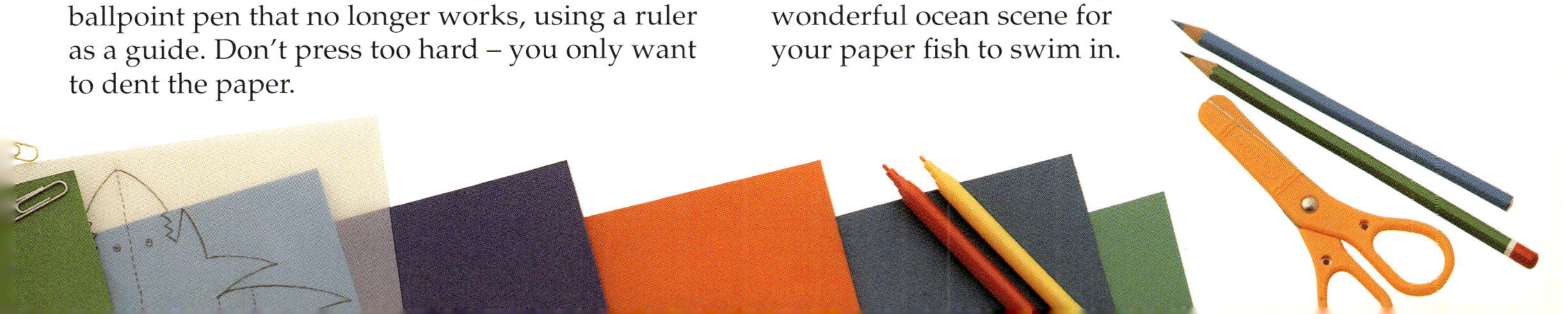

# Colorful Coral Reef Fish

Corals are brightly-colored sea creatures that grow in warm, shallow waters. They look like plants, but they are in fact animals which grow in large groups and share a common, brittle skeleton.

The fish that live around the coral reef are very brightly-colored so they blend with their exotic surroundings. There is a huge variety of fish with unusual shapes, colors, patterns, and sizes. The coral reef is like a big, bright, underwater city, teeming with life.

Follow the instructions on pages 4 and 5 to trace, cut out, and crease a paper fish pattern. Then follow the steps opposite to fold your fish. Decorate your model and sharpen any creases between your fingernails.

**You will need**

Tracing paper and pencil
Stiff colored paper
Paper clips
Scissors and ruler
Knitting needle or old ballpoint pen
Paper glue
Colored markers, pencil crayons, or crayons
Nylon thread and clear tape

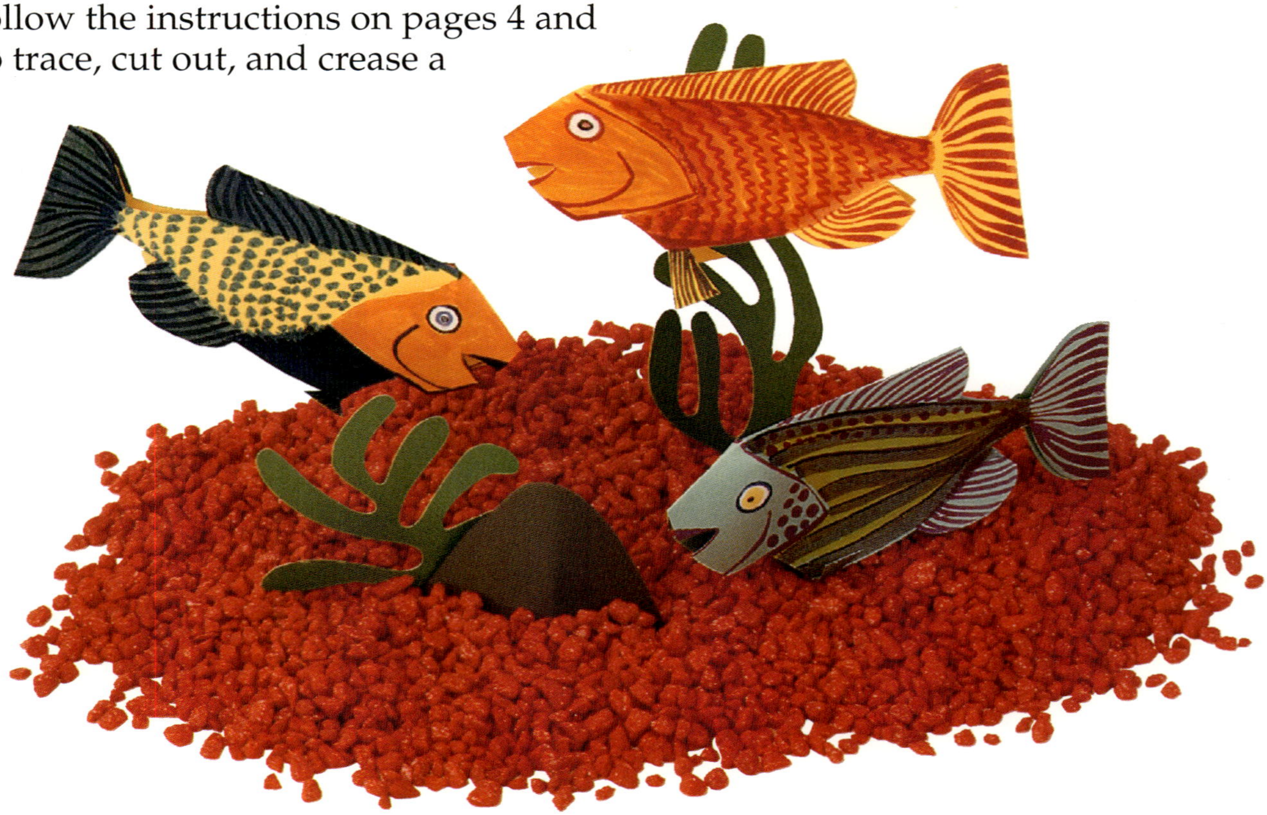

## FOLDING YOUR FISH

1 When you have cut out a paper fish pattern and creased the fold lines, fold the fish in half along the center line.

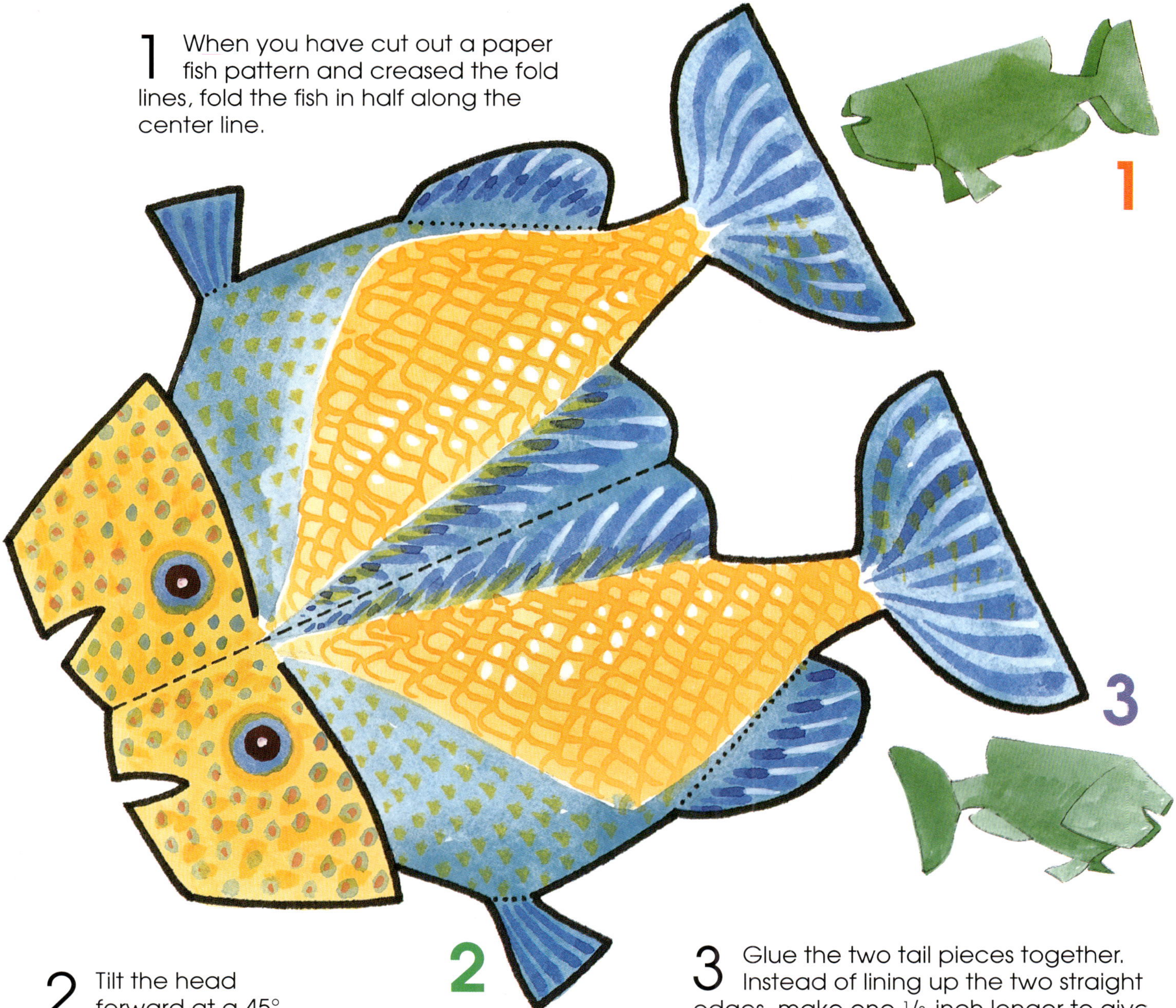

1

3

2

2 Tilt the head forward at a 45° angle and add a dab of glue on each side between the head and body, to hold the head in place.

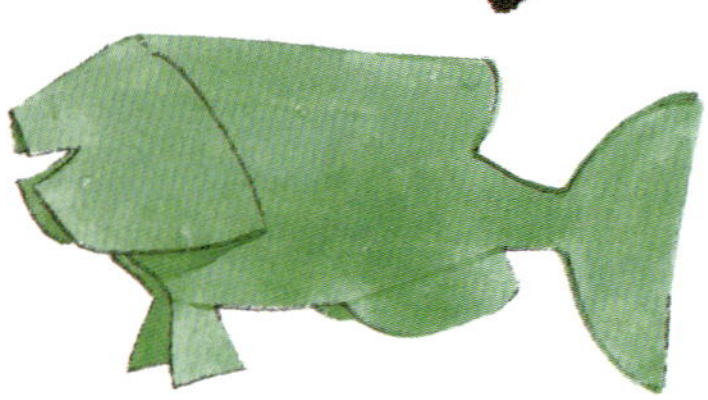

3 Glue the two tail pieces together. Instead of lining up the two straight edges, make one 1/8 inch longer to give the tail a realistic swishing curve. Angle the fins away from the body and then decorate your coral reef fish. Tape a piece of nylon thread to the back of your fish to hang it from.

# Basking Gray Seals

Although seals can be seen on the shores of cooler countries, they spend most of their lives in the water. Because they breathe air like we do, they have to come to the surface every few minutes, even while they are asleep.

Seals evolved from land creatures and today's seals still have back limbs in the form of flippers. They use their flippers to push themselves along on land, and tuck them back to form a steering rudder when they swim.

Follow the instructions on pages 4 and 5 to trace, cut out, and crease a paper seal pattern. Fold your pattern into a 3-D model following the steps opposite. Lay it out flat to decorate it and then refold your model, sharpening the creases between your fingernails.

**You will need**

Tracing paper and pencil
Stiff colored paper
Paper clips
Scissors and ruler
Knitting needle or old ballpoint pen
Colored markers, pencil crayons, or crayons

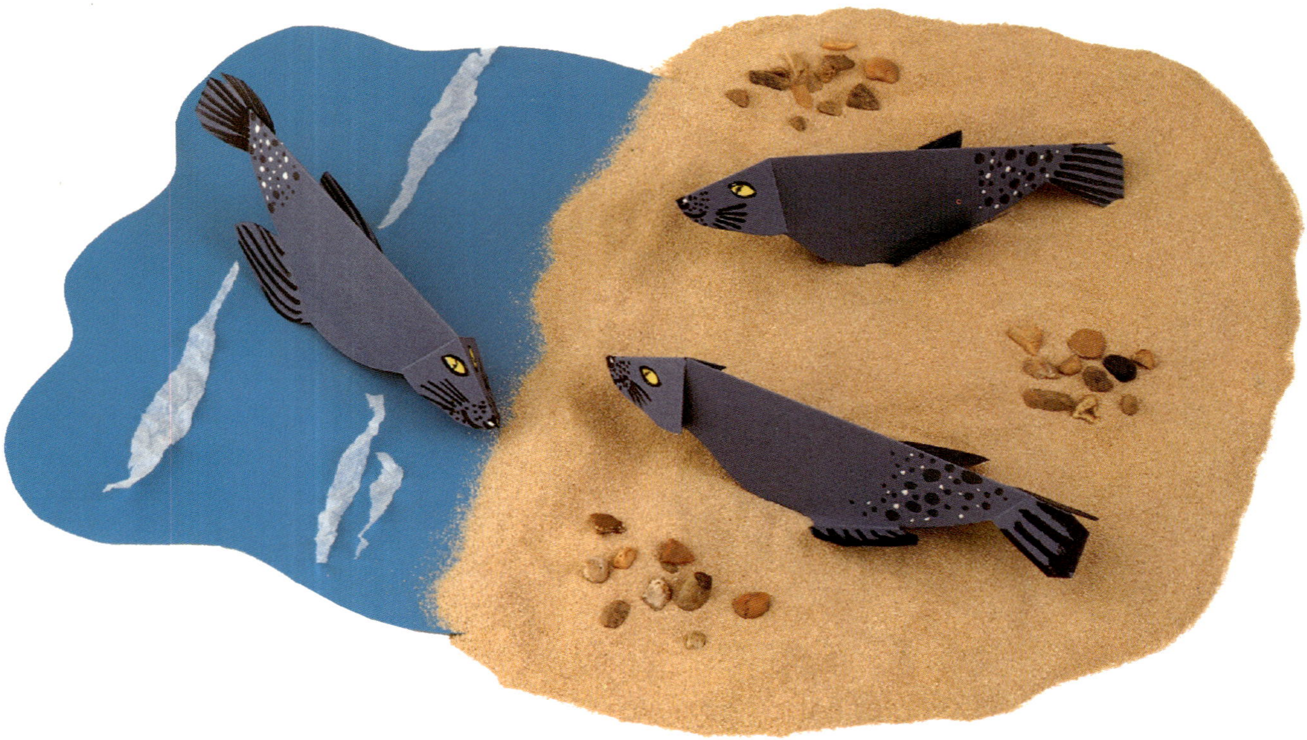

## FOLDING YOUR SEAL

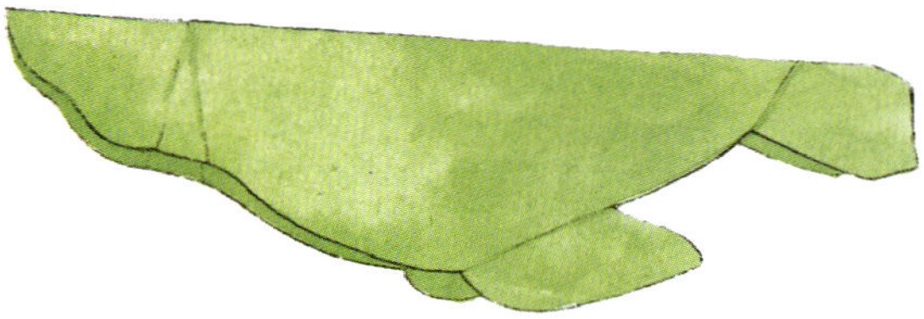

1

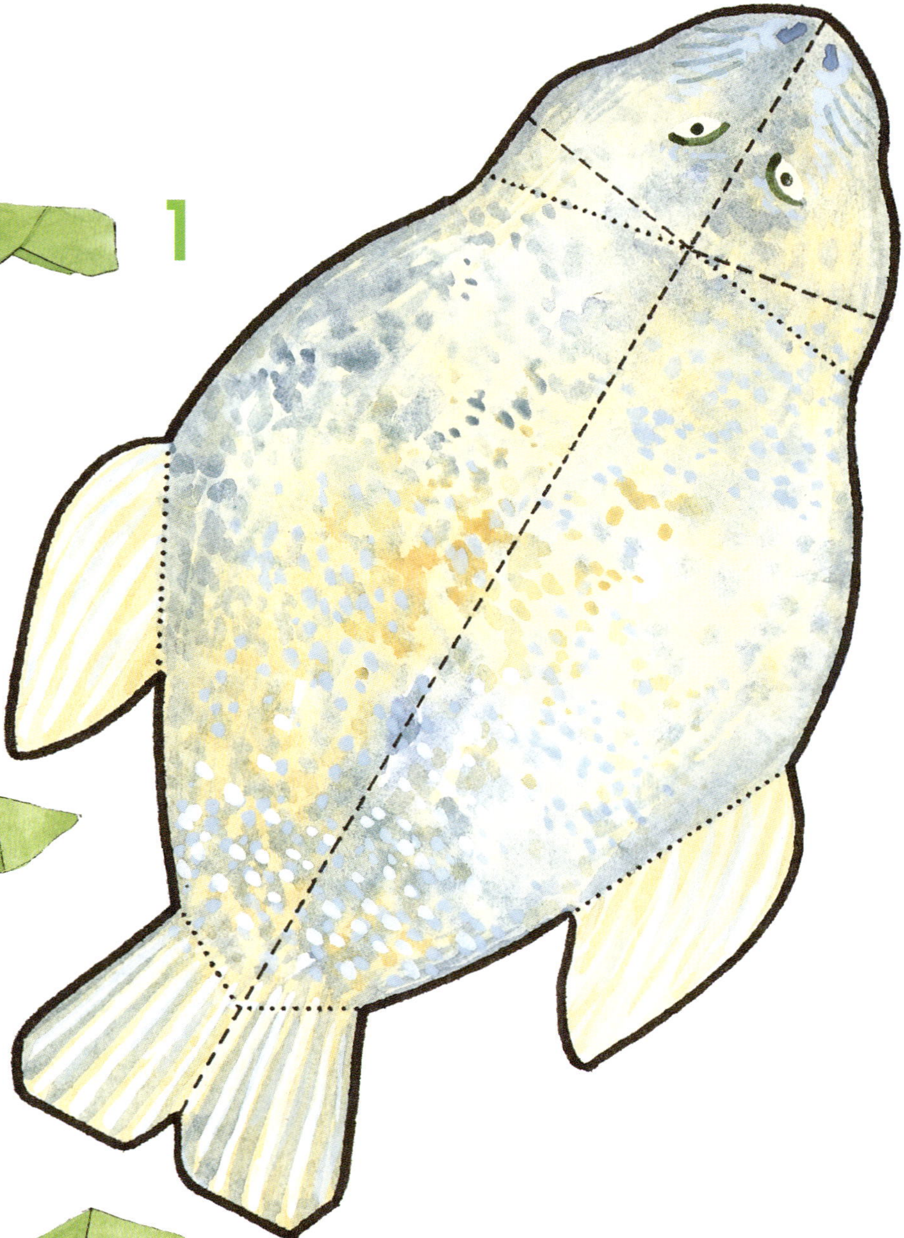

1 When you have cut out a paper seal pattern and creased all the fold lines, fold the seal in half along the center line.

2

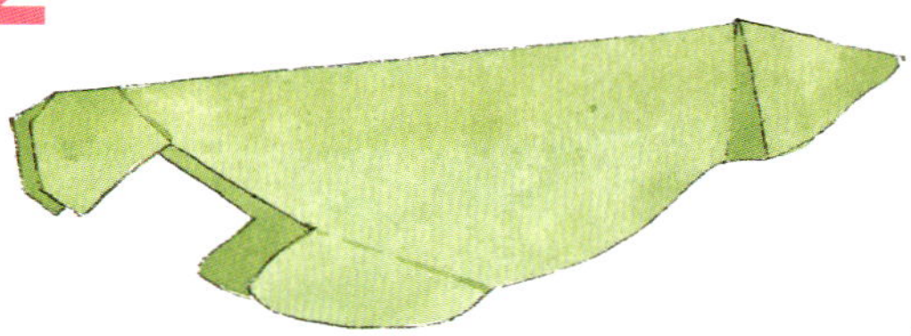

2 Make the triangular folds at the back of the head to tilt the head forward. Fold dashed lines upward and dotted lines downward.

3

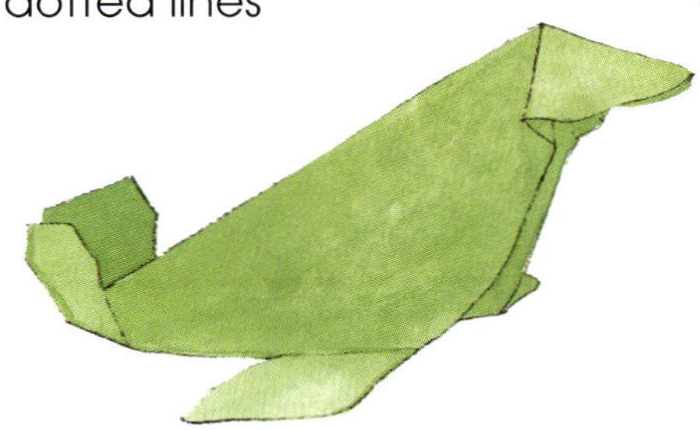

3 Fold the tail flippers upward and fold out the front flippers at right angles to the body.

# Seaside Starfish

Starfish are strange creatures. They have five identical arms, each with a groove of suckers on the underside.

The starfish's mouth is in the center where all the grooves meet and when it eats, the starfish pushes its stomach outside its body to swallow and digest its food.

A starfish can open clams using its arms to pull the shells apart. It eats the soft, tasty meat inside.

Follow the instructions on pages 4 and 5 to trace, cut out, and crease a paper starfish pattern. Fold it into a 3-D model following the steps opposite. Decorate your model and sharpen any creases between your fingernails.

**You will need**

Tracing paper and pencil
Stiff colored paper
Paper clips
Scissors and ruler
Knitting needle or ballpoint pen
Colored markers, pencil crayons, or crayons
White paint and paintbrush

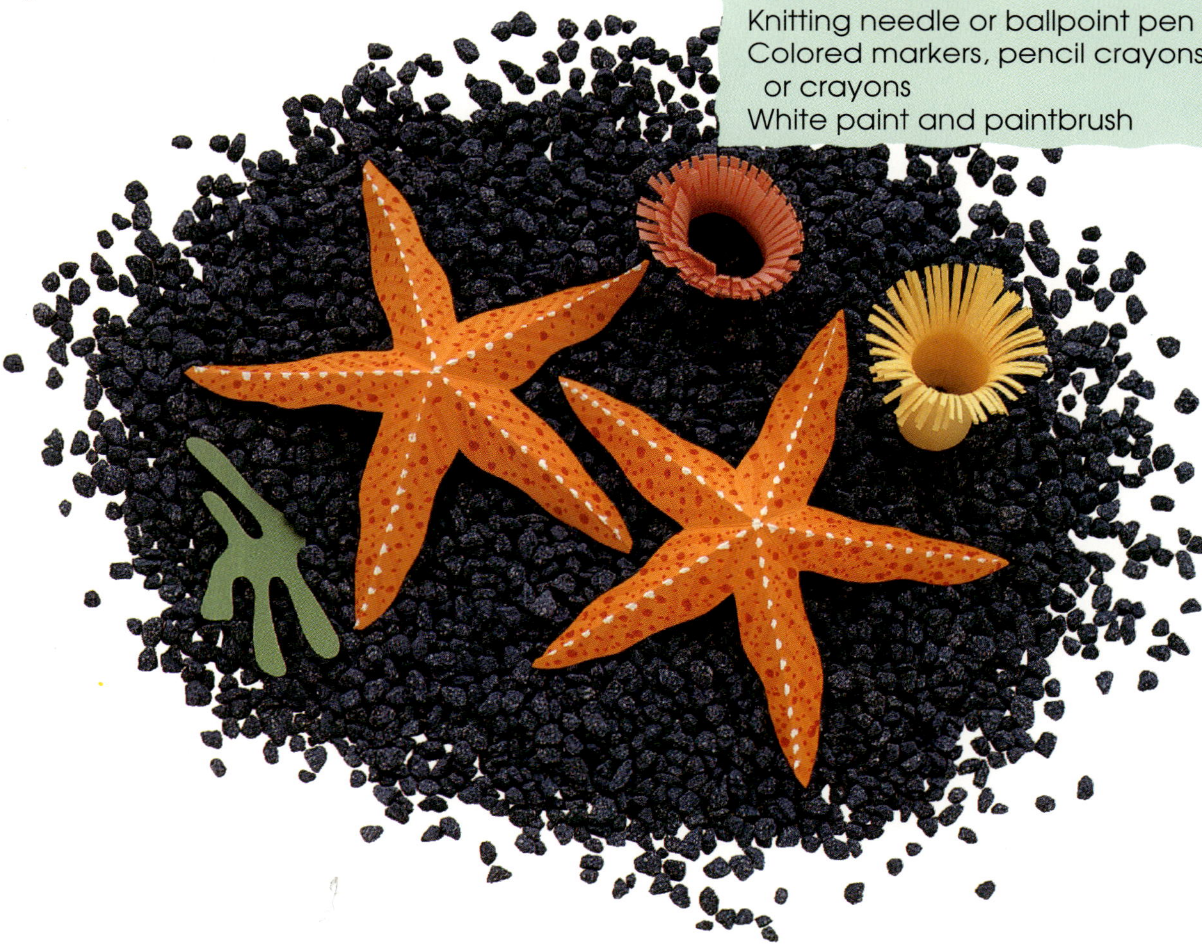

## FOLDING YOUR STARFISH

1

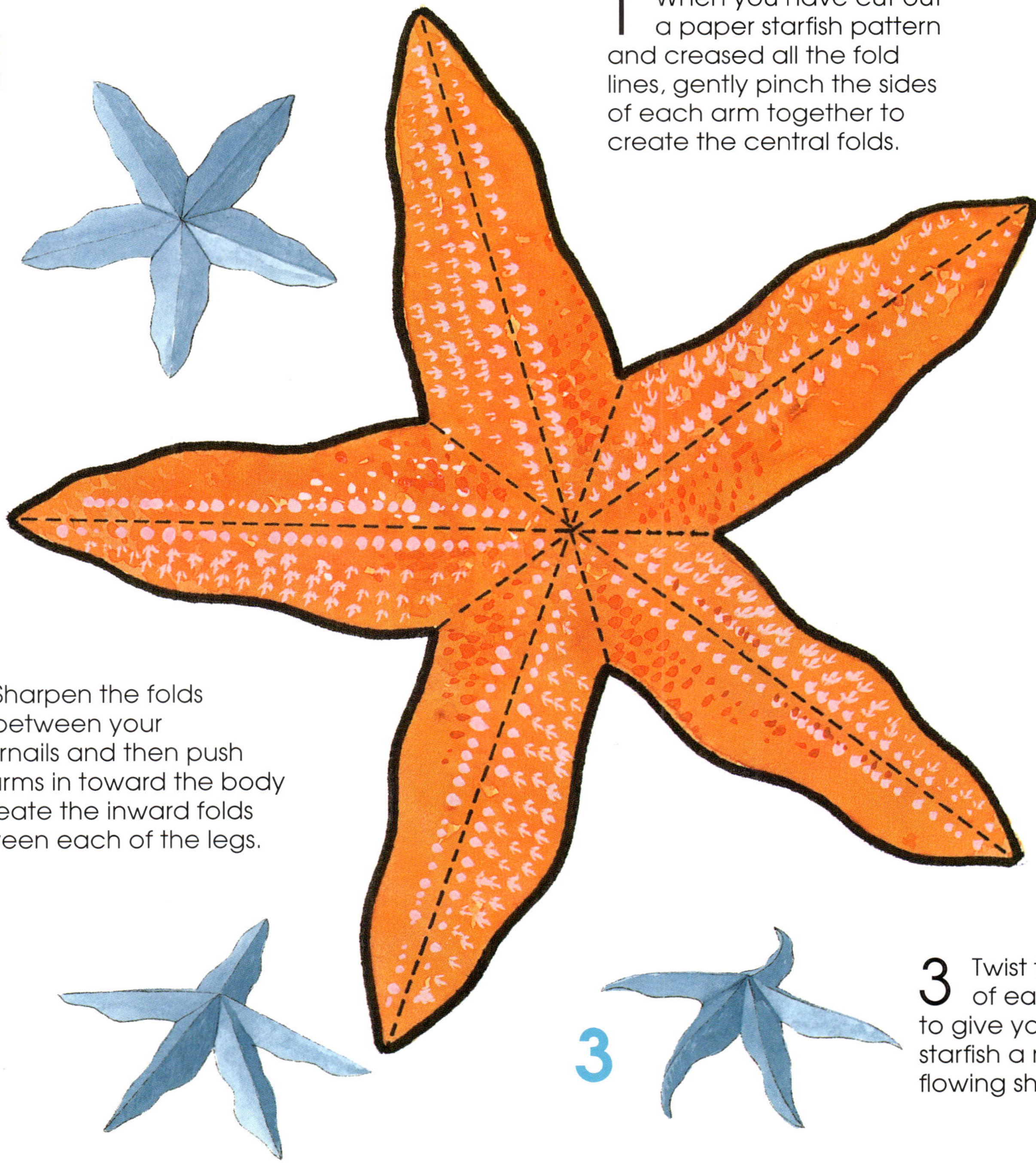

1 When you have cut out a paper starfish pattern and creased all the fold lines, gently pinch the sides of each arm together to create the central folds.

2 Sharpen the folds between your fingernails and then push the arms in toward the body to create the inward folds between each of the legs.

2

3

3 Twist the end of each arm to give your starfish a natural, flowing shape.

# Friendly Dolphins

Dolphins are not fish, but mammals like us. They live in the sea, but come to the surface to breathe air. They are graceful, athletic creatures and can swim very fast, leap high out of the water, and surf along the waves.

Dolphins are very intelligent and have a highly-developed language which enables them to speak to one another.

Sound is very important to the dolphin. It tracks its food using sonar. It sends out sounds which hit against other sea creatures. The dolphin can then judge the position of its prey by the echo it sends back.

Follow the instructions on pages 4 and 5 to trace, cut out, and crease a paper dolphin pattern. Fold it into a 3-D model following the steps opposite. Lay it flat to decorate it and refold your model and sharpen the creases.

**You will need**

Tracing paper and pencil
Stiff colored paper
Paper clips
Scissors and ruler
Knitting needle or old ballpoint pen
Craft knife (for adult use only)
Colored markers, pencil crayons, or crayons
Nylon thread and clear tape

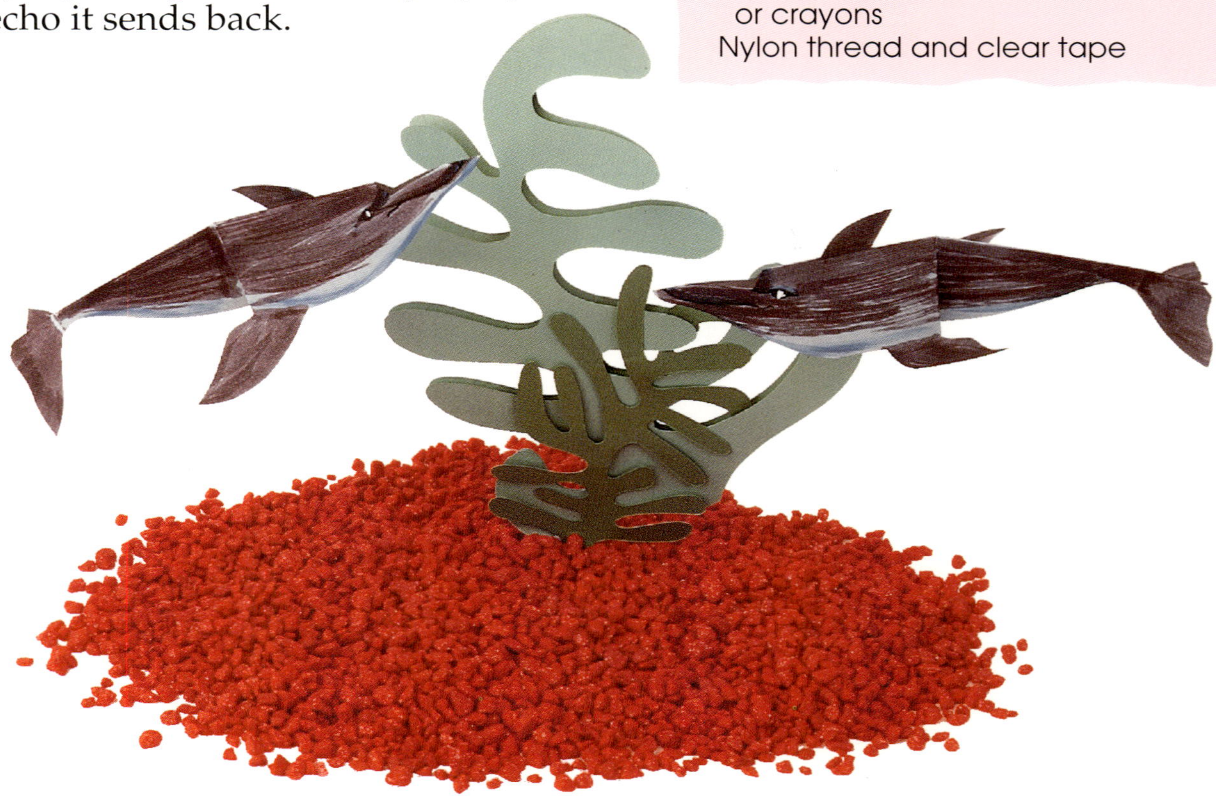

## FOLDING YOUR DOLPHIN

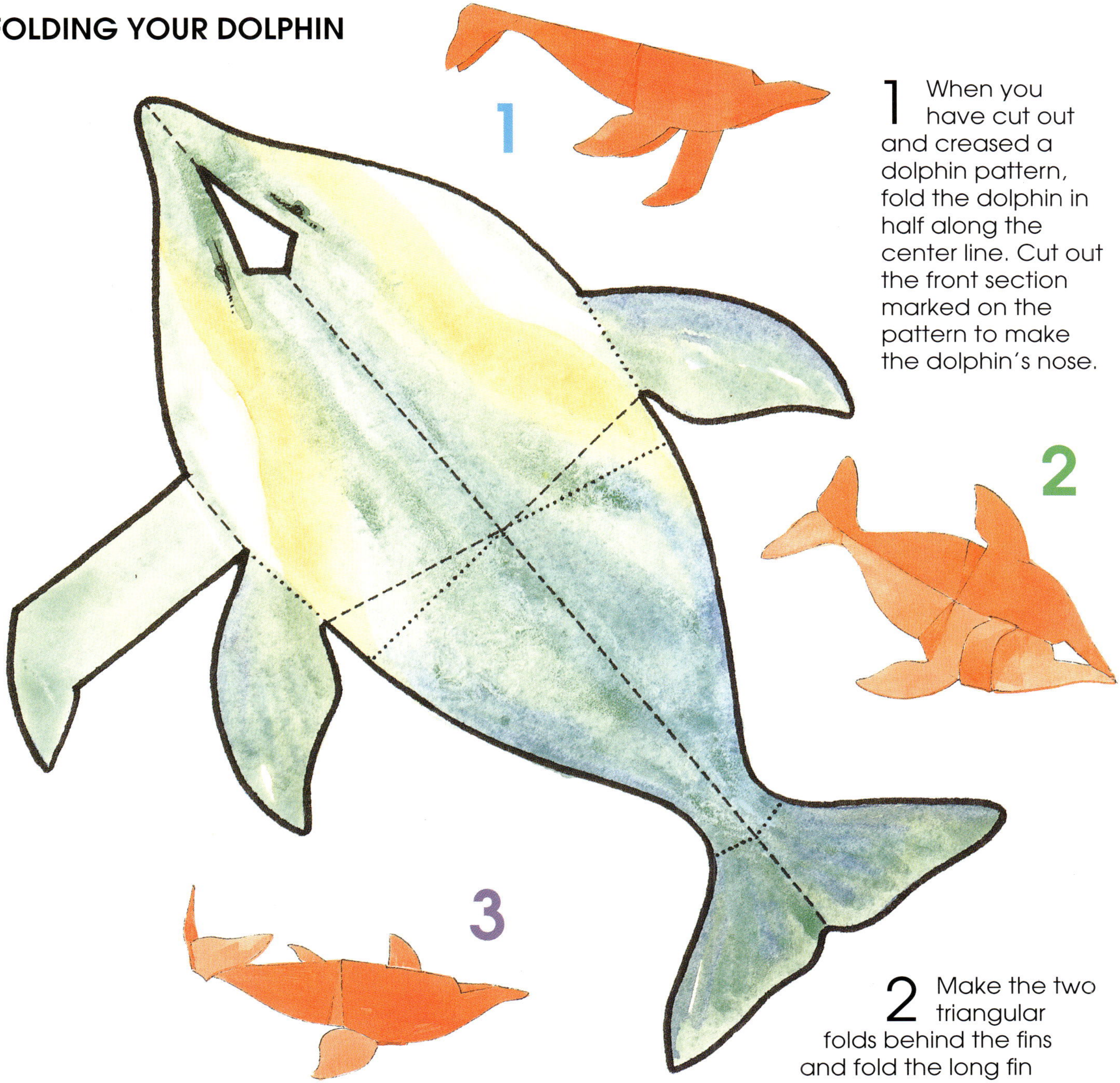

1

1 When you have cut out and creased a dolphin pattern, fold the dolphin in half along the center line. Cut out the front section marked on the pattern to make the dolphin's nose.

2

3

2 Make the two triangular folds behind the fins and fold the long fin inward. Ask an adult to cut the slit along the center fold line, using a craft knife. Tuck the fin up through the slit.

3 Fold the tail upward and bend out the two side fins. Tape a piece of nylon thread to the back of the dolphin to hang it from.

# Curly-tentacled Octopus

The octopus belongs to a family known as mollusks and is related to the slug.

It has eight tentacles with rows of suckers running along them. It uses its tentacles to grab passing food, such as crabs and lobsters, and feed it into its powerful beaklike mouth.

The octopus hides in underground caves and moves around by sucking up water and shooting it out again with great force. When under attack, the octopus can squirt out a jet of an inklike substance that clouds the water and allows the octopus to sneak away.

Follow the instructions on pages 4 and 5 to trace, cut out, and crease a paper octopus pattern. Then follow the steps opposite to fold the pattern into a 3-D model. Lay it flat to decorate it and then refold it, sharpening the creases between your fingernails.

### You will need

Tracing paper and pencil
Stiff colored paper
Paper clips
Scissors and ruler
Knitting needle or old ballpoint pen
Colored markers, pencil crayons, or crayons
Paper glue

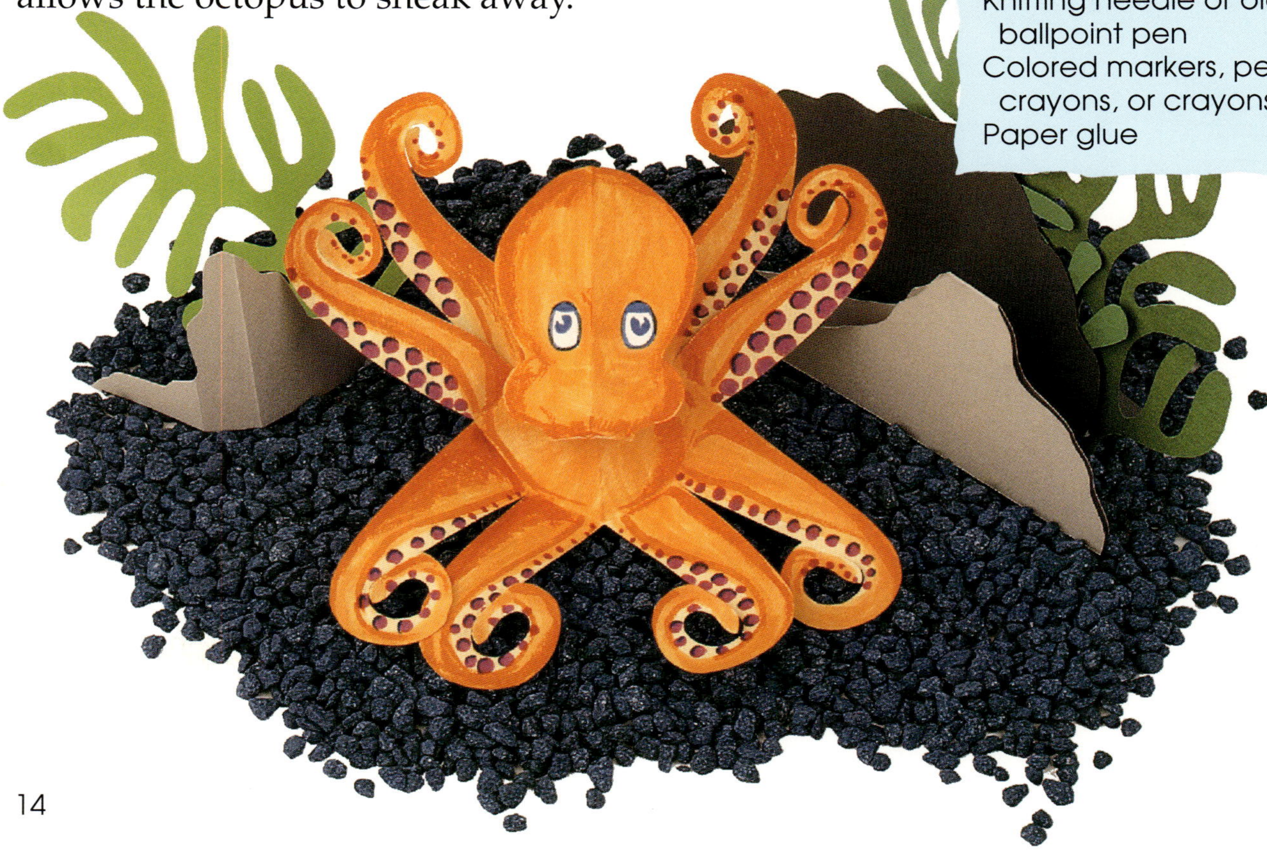

## FOLDING YOUR OCTOPUS

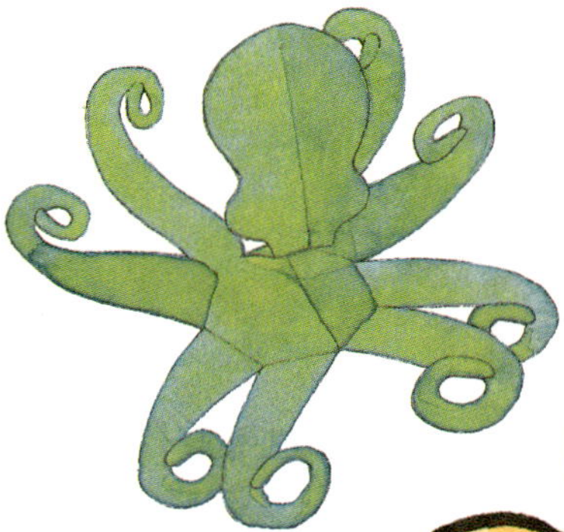

1

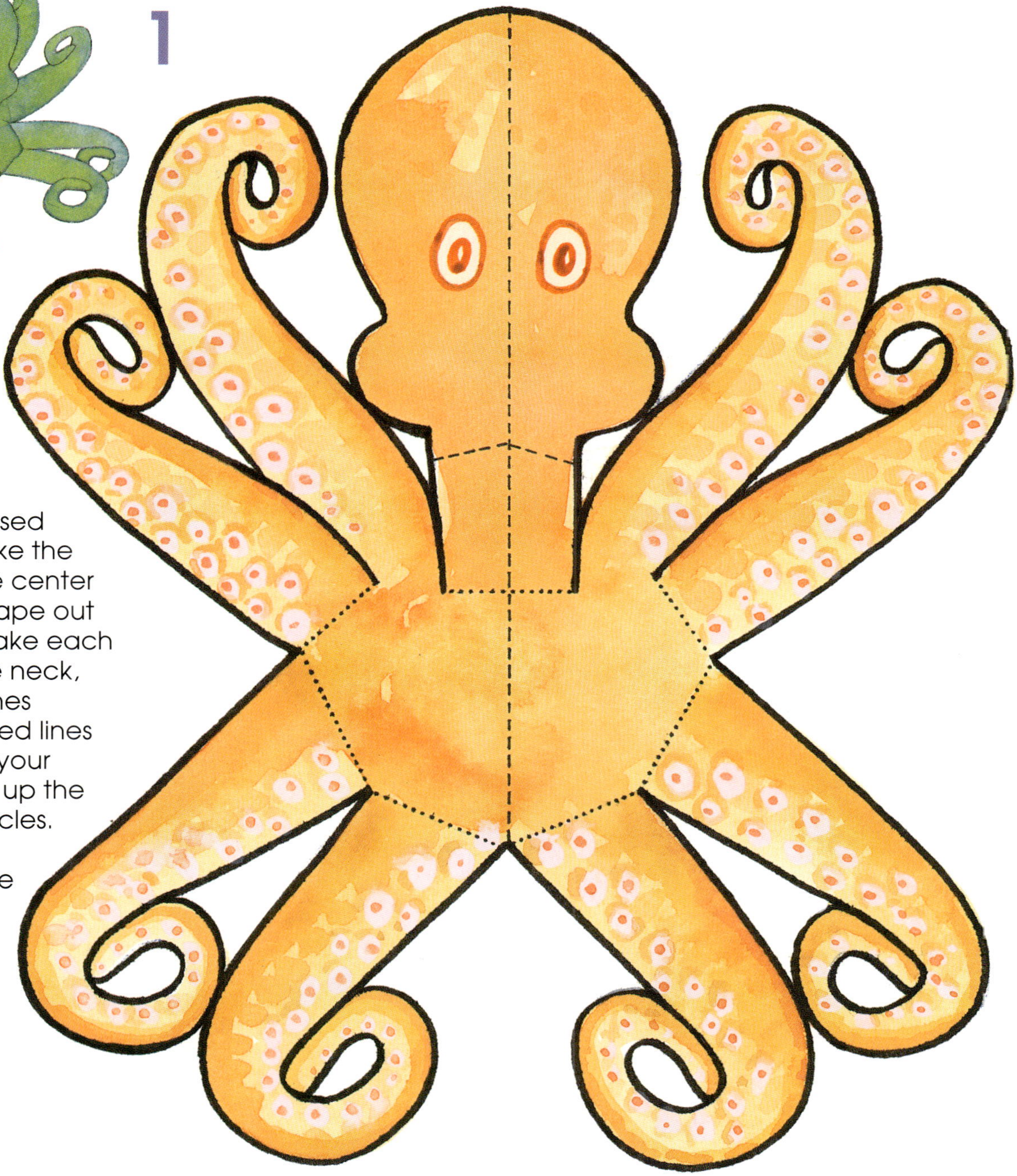

1 When you have cut out a paper octopus pattern and creased the fold lines, make the first fold down the center line. Open the shape out flat again and make each of the folds at the neck, folding dashed lines upward and dotted lines down. Decorate your octopus and curl up the ends of the tentacles. You may want to add a dab of glue between the neck and the body to keep the head upright.

# Shimmering Rays

These flat-bodied fish are related to sharks. They spend most of their time on the ocean bed, feeding on shellfish.

There are many different types of ray, the largest being the manta ray which can measure up to 20 feet wide.

One of the most fearsome is the sting ray. Its tail has a ragged spear which can inflict a deadly wound. Other rays attack their prey by giving it an electric shock.

Follow the instructions on pages 4 and 5 to trace, cut out, and crease a paper ray shape. Follow the steps opposite to fold your ray. Decorate your model and sharpen up the creases between your fingernails.

**You will need**

Tracing paper and pencil
Stiff colored paper
Paper clips
Scissors and ruler
Knitting needle or old ballpoint pen
Craft knife (for adult use only)
Colored markers, pencil crayons, or crayons

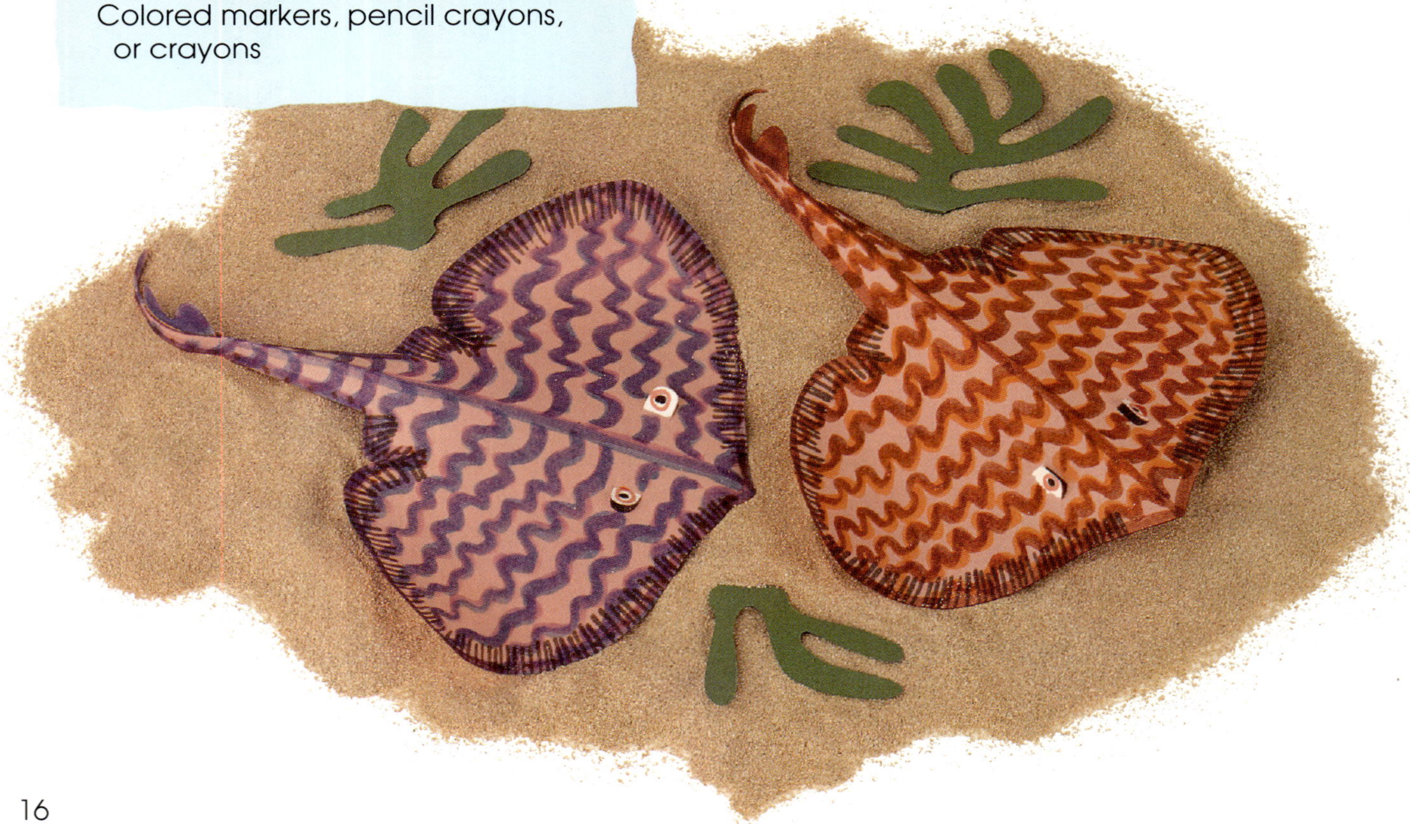

## FOLDING YOUR RAY

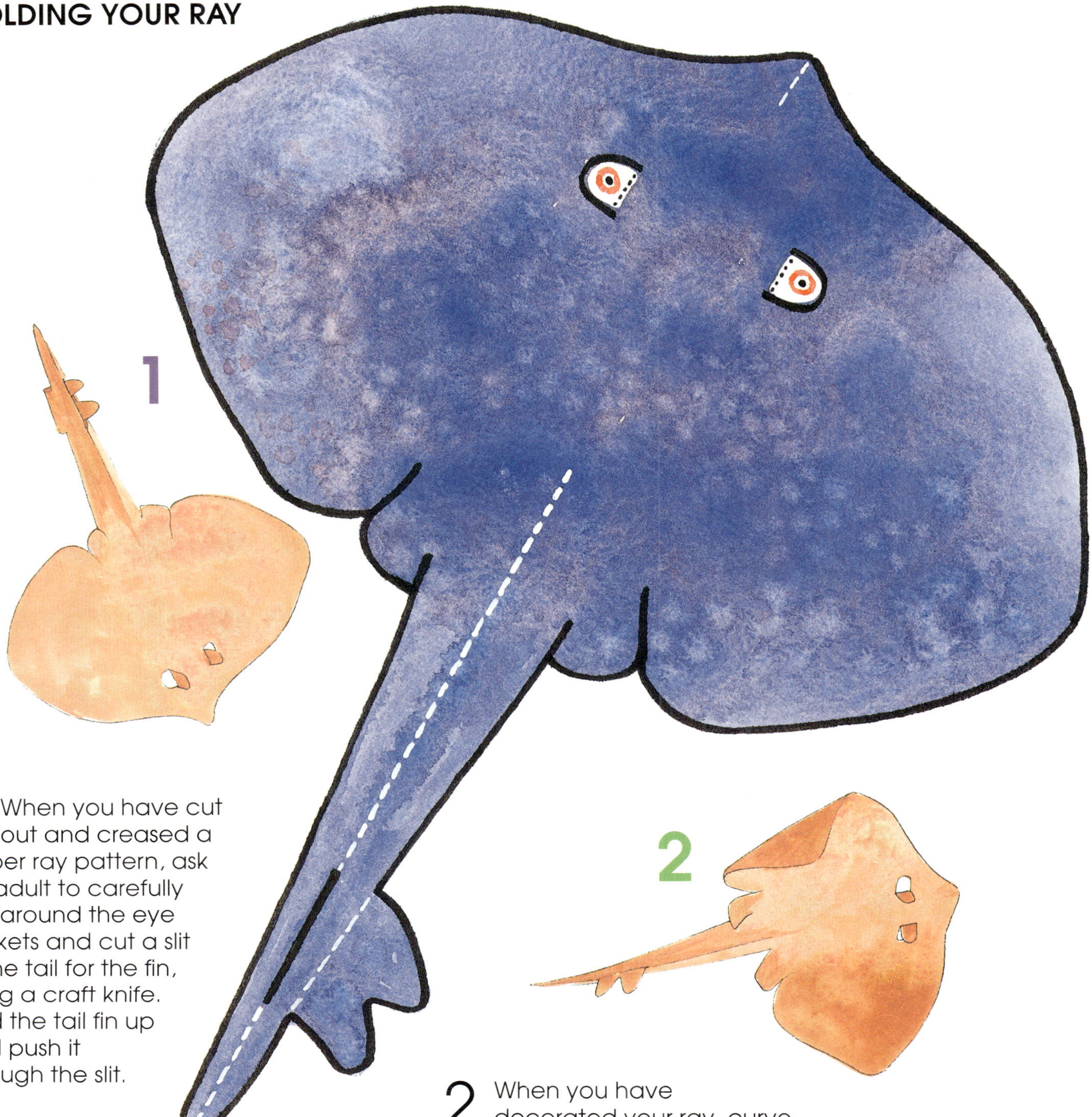

1

2

1 When you have cut out and creased a paper ray pattern, ask an adult to carefully cut around the eye sockets and cut a slit in the tail for the fin, using a craft knife. Fold the tail fin up and push it through the slit.

2 When you have decorated your ray, curve the edges to give the ray a rounded, floating shape.

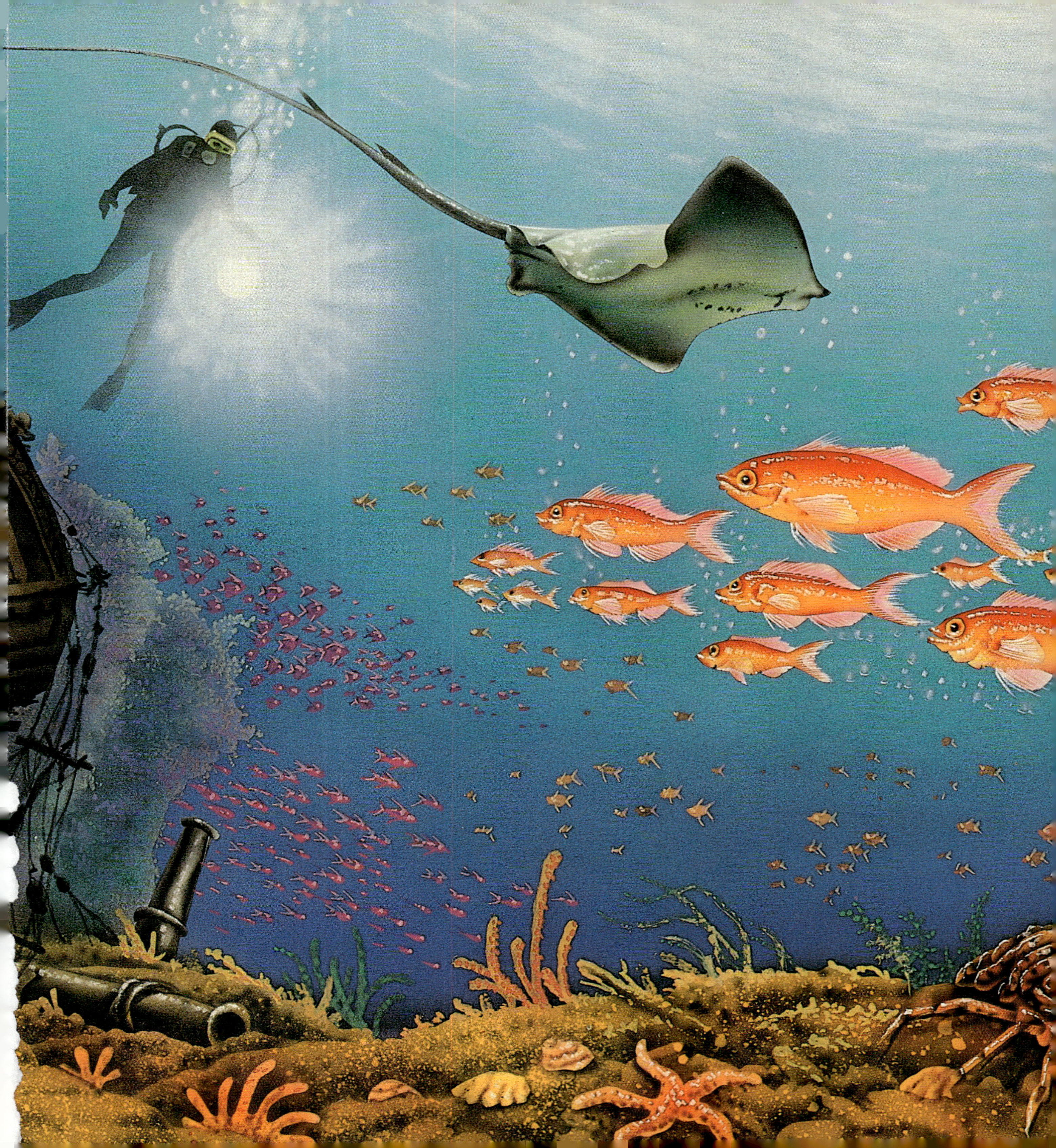

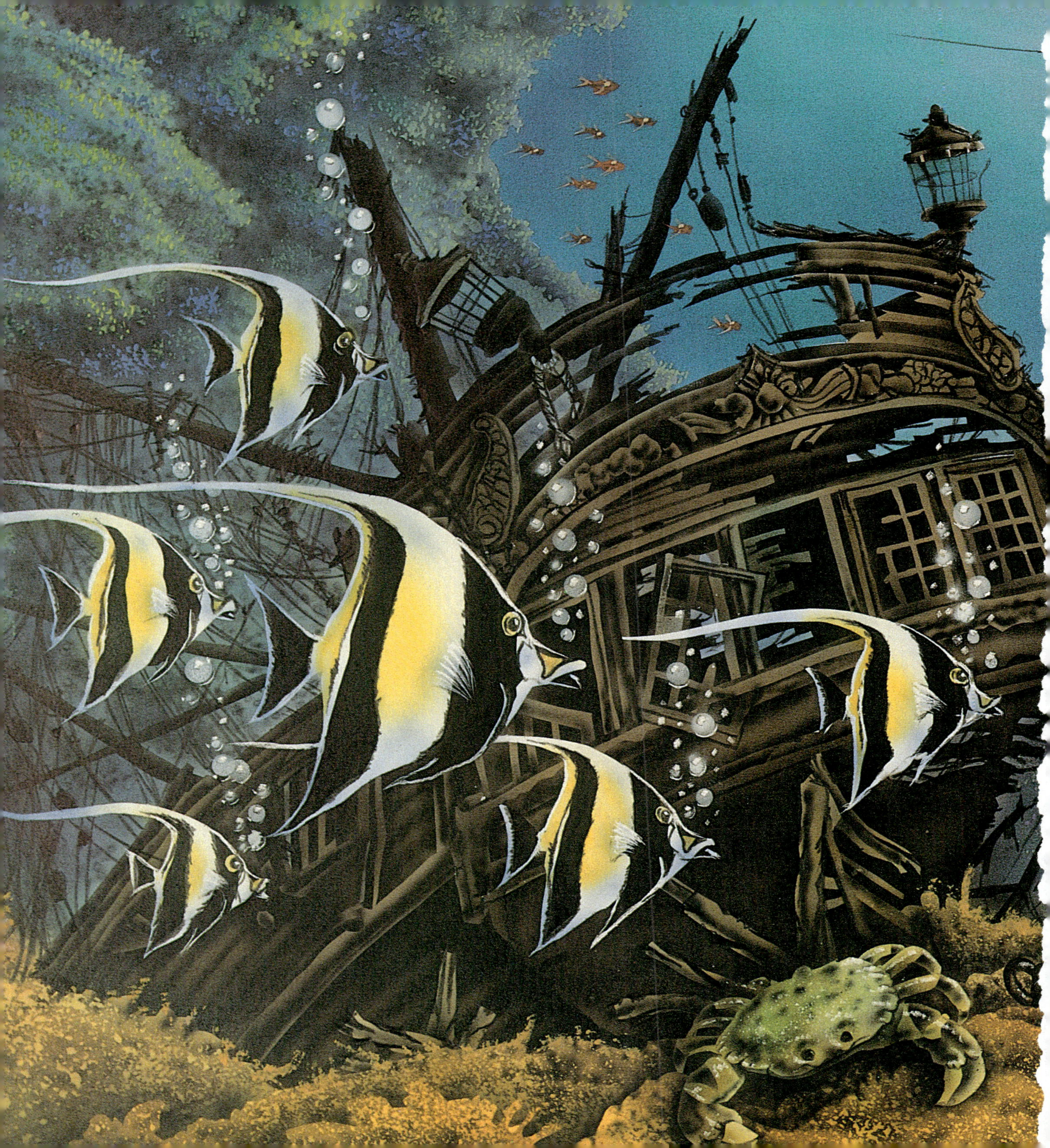

# Scenery to Make

Simple scenery is easy to make and can be used to create exciting settings for an underwater scene.

Follow the instructions on pages 4 and 5 to transfer the patterns here onto colored paper. You can make longer lengths of corals and rocks by tracing the same pattern several times, joining one onto the next.

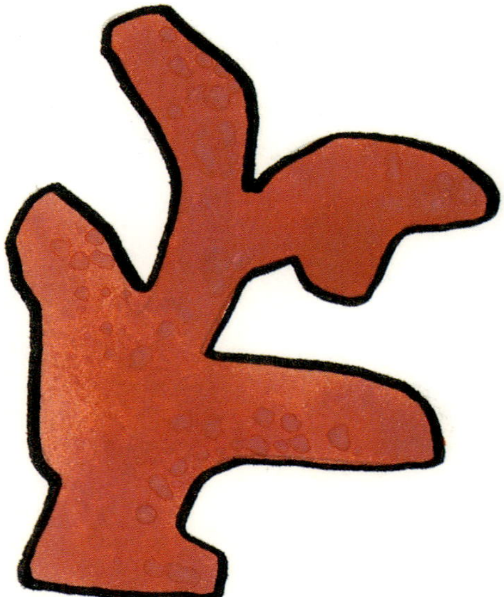

coral

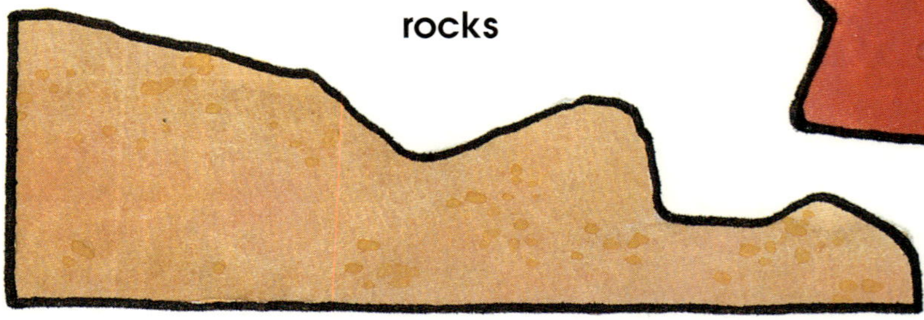

rocks

a

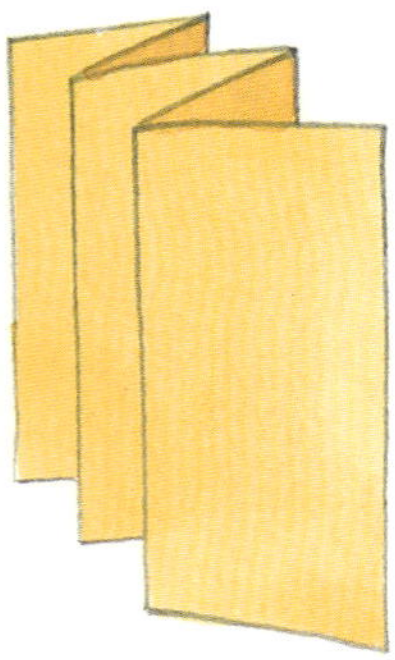

b

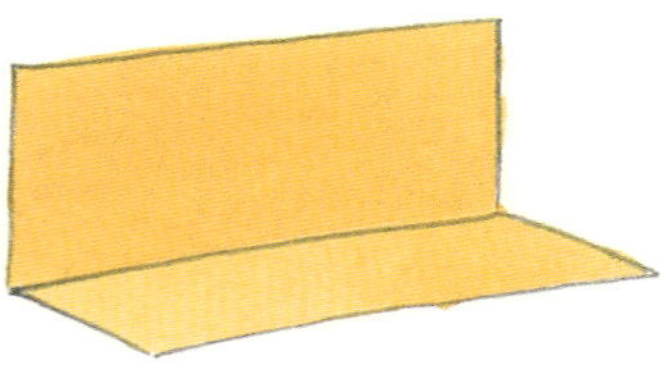

c

## FOLDING YOUR FOLIAGE

There are three main ways to fold scenery. Once you have traced the shapes, transferred them onto colored paper, and cut them out, fold the patterns in one of the following ways:

*(a)* Fold the shape in half down the center to make it stand upright.

*(b)* Fold the shape backward and forward, concertina-style to make a string of rocks or corals.

*(c)* Make one or more right-angled folds to form a box shape for rocks or corals.

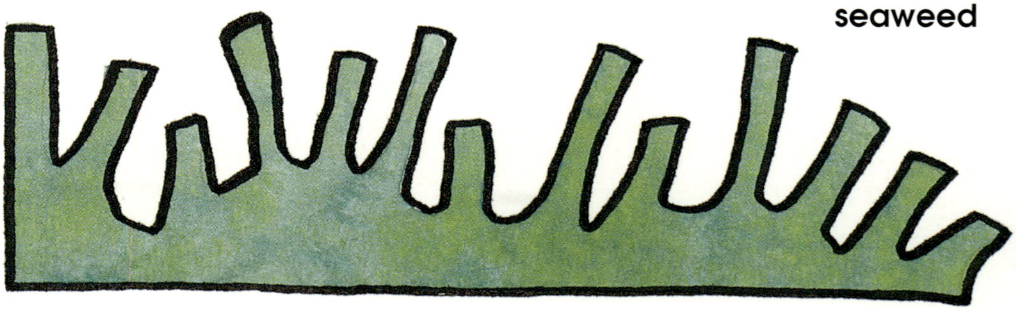

corals and seaweed

Make longer lengths of rocks or corals by tracing the same pattern several times in a joined-up row. Use the folding styles on the opposite page to create different looks.

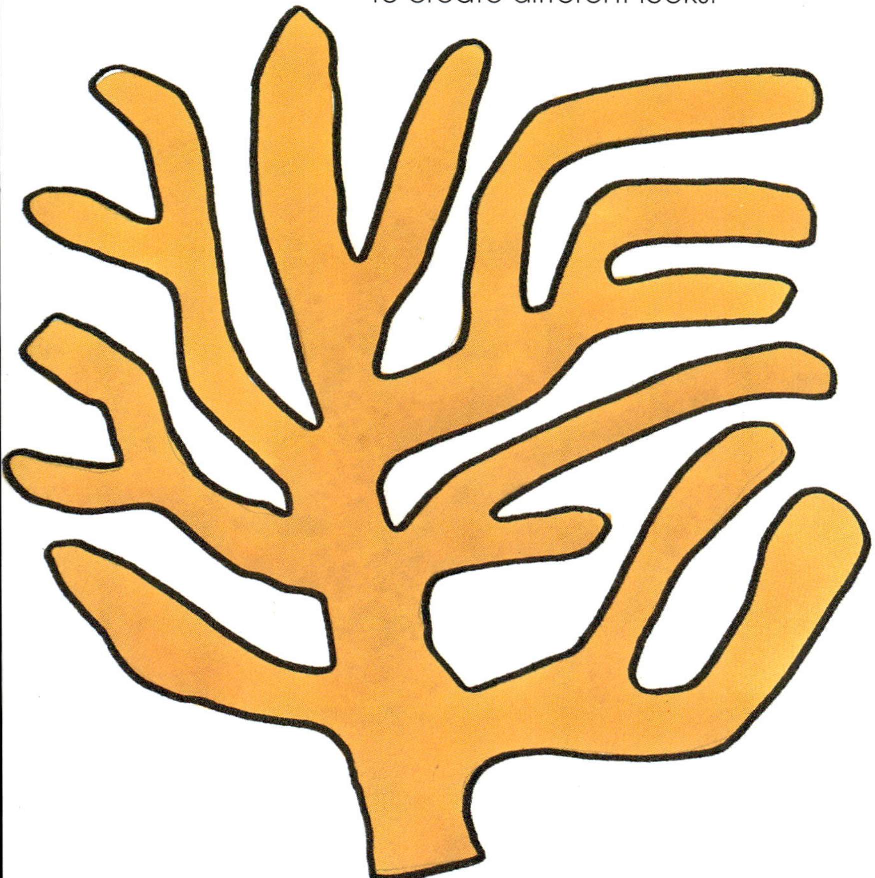

**sea anenome**

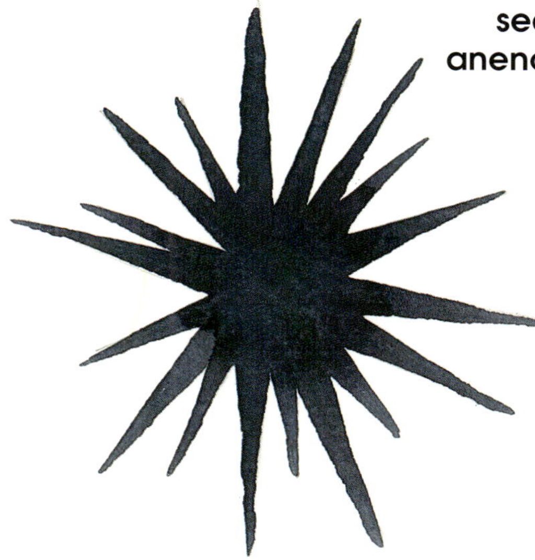

Cut small pieces of coral, seaweed, or individual sea anenomes out of colored paper. Tape a piece of nylon thread to the back of each and hang them in front of your ocean scene. Or simply stand them on the seabed.

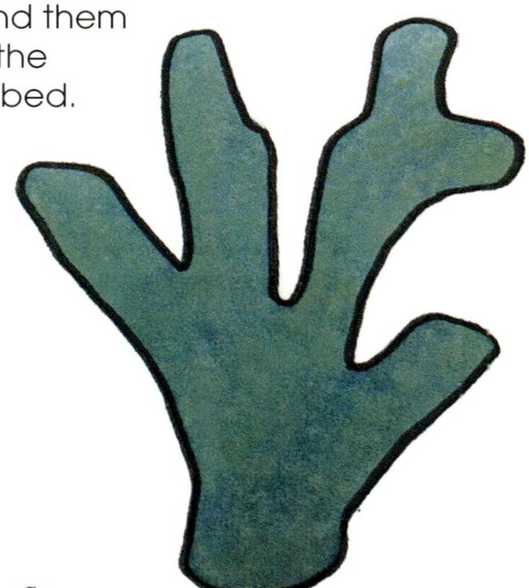

**seaweed and corals**

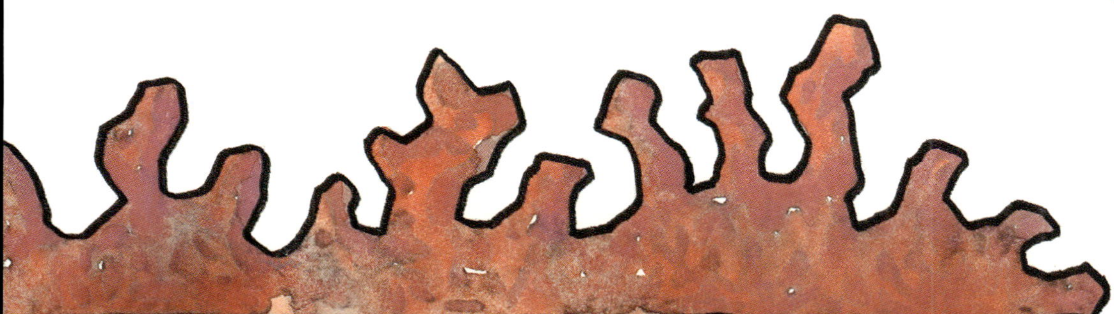

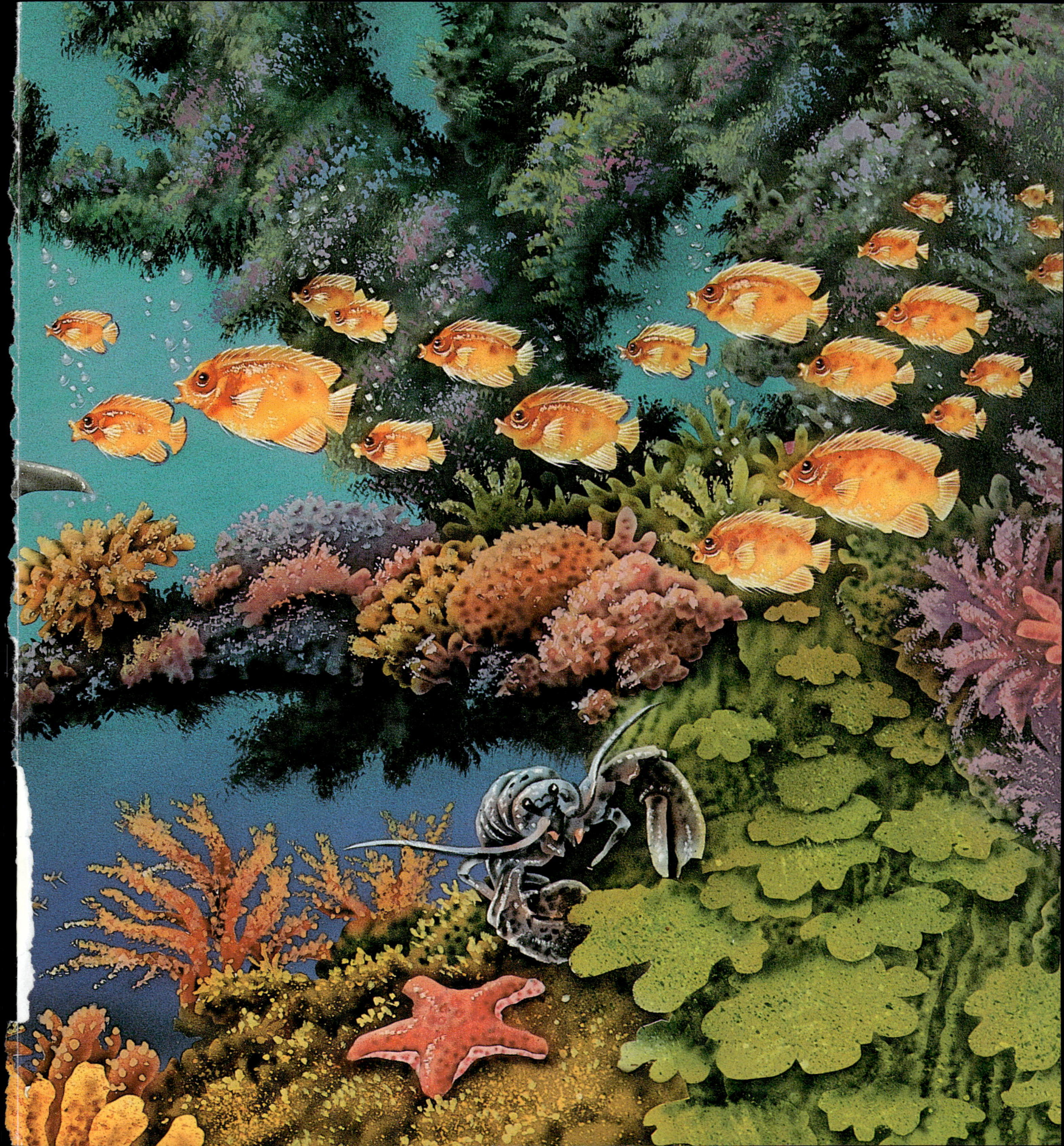

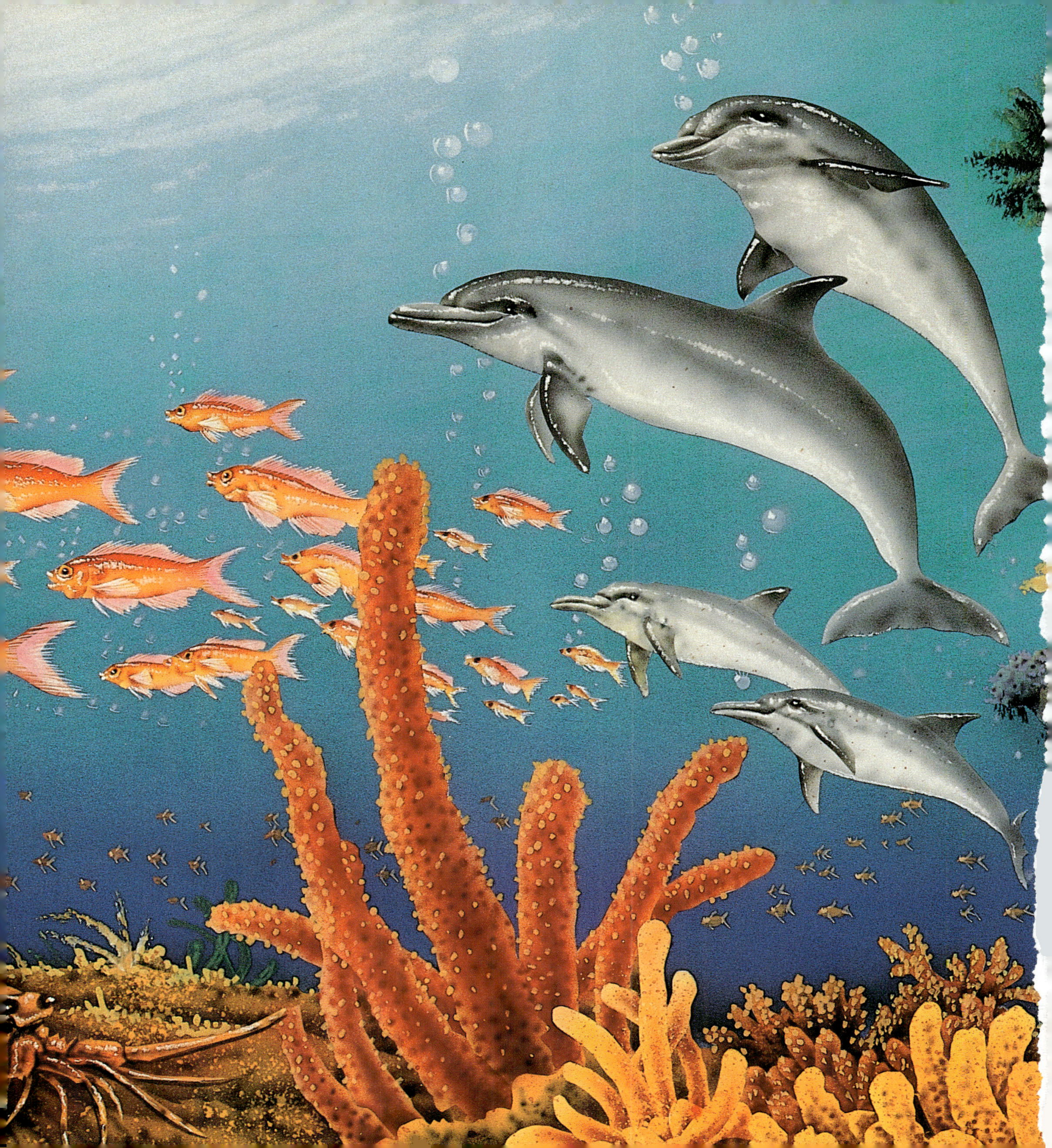

# Creeping Crabs

Crabs are anthropods, which means that they are creatures with jointed legs.

There are over 4, 000 different species of crab, which come in all shapes and sizes. They can measure as little as 1/4 inch across or as large as 12 inches.

Although there are some freshwater crabs, most live in the sea and are scavengers which feed on the remains of dead sea creatures. Some eat seaweed while others crush live mussels with their powerful claws and eat the soft meat inside.

Follow the instructions on pages 4 and 5 to trace, cut out, and crease a paper crab pattern. Then follow the steps opposite to fold your crab into a 3-D model. Open it out flat to decorate it and then refold it, sharpening all the creases between your fingernails.

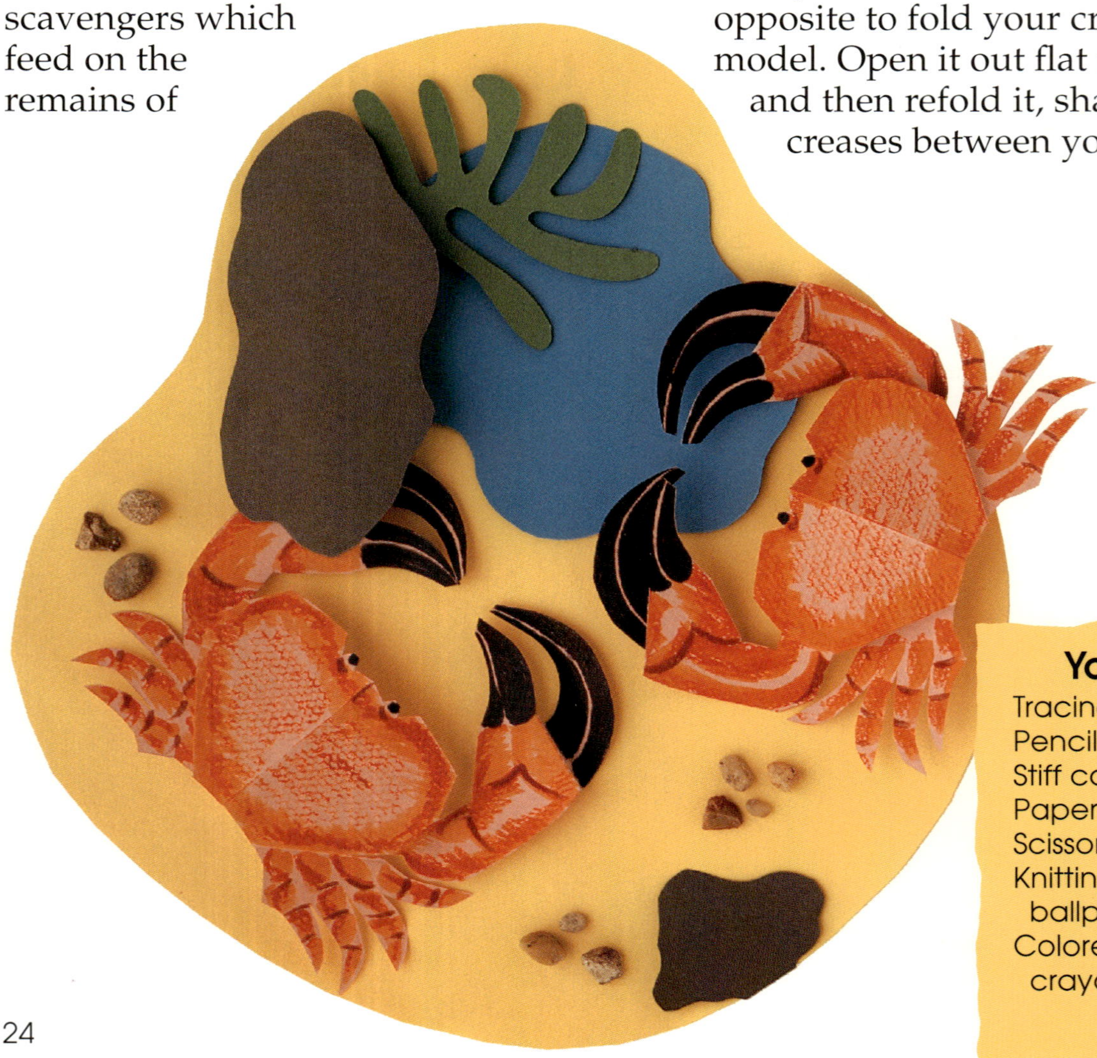

**You will need**

- Tracing paper
- Pencil
- Stiff colored paper
- Paper clips
- Scissors and ruler
- Knitting needle or old ballpoint pen
- Colored markers, pencil crayons, or crayons

## FOLDING YOUR CRAB

1 When you have cut out and creased a paper crab pattern, fold the body lightly down the middle, along the center fold line.

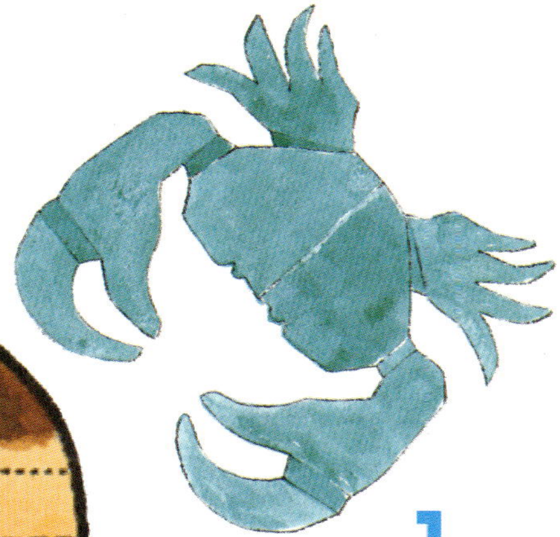

1

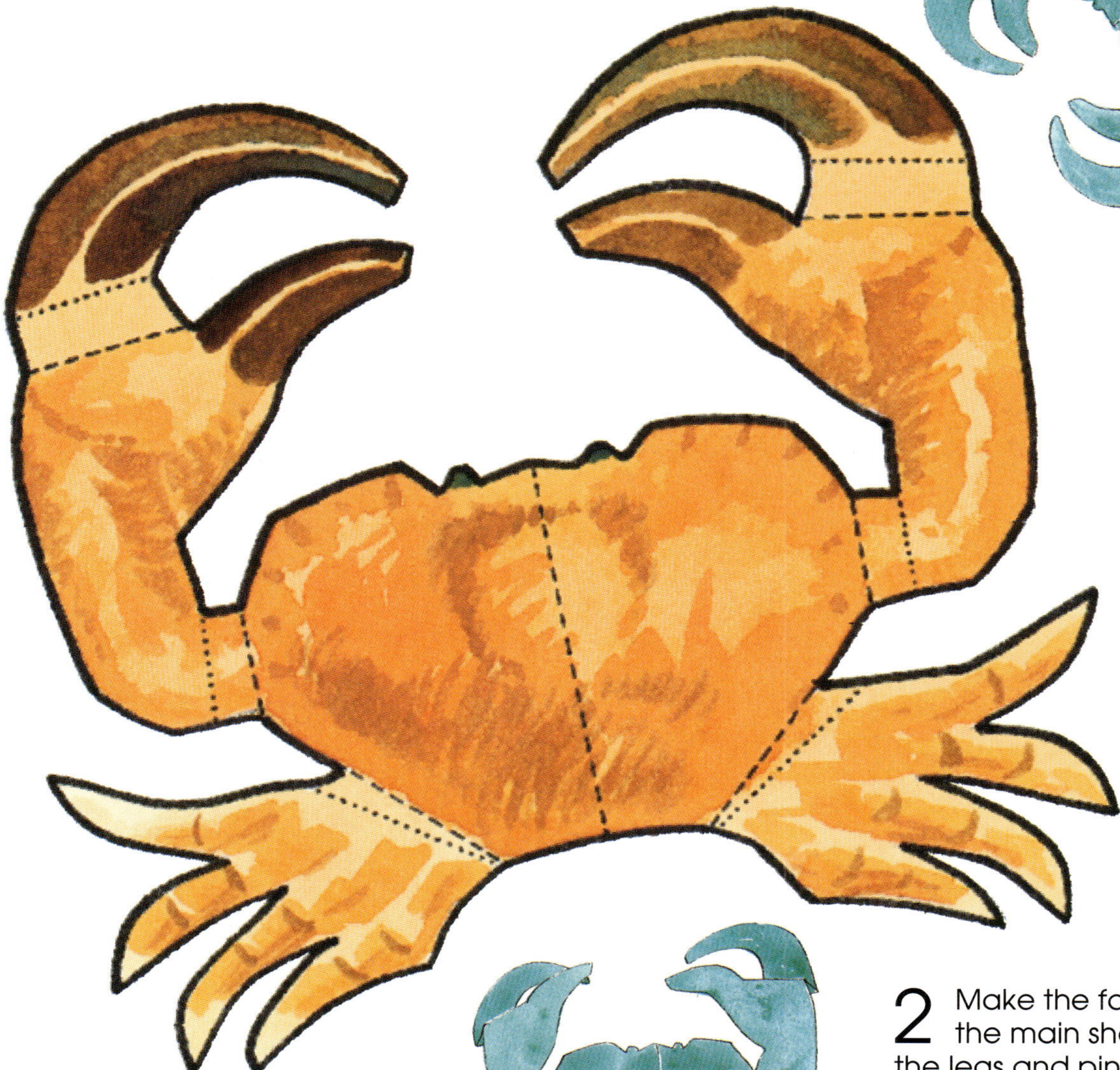

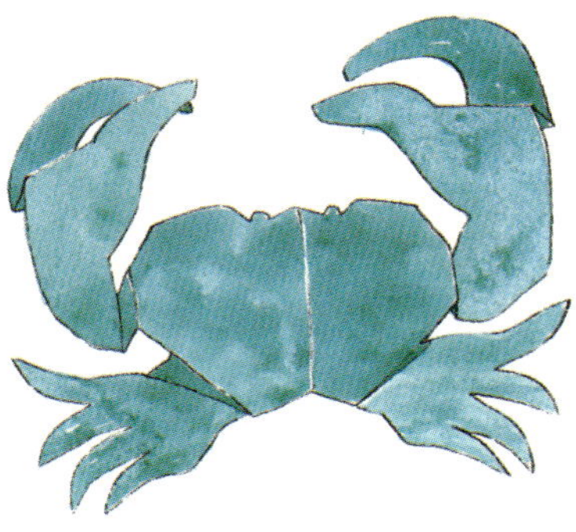

2

2 Make the folds that lift the main shell up from the legs and pincers, folding dashed lines upward and dotted lines down. Make the inward folds on the pincers, and bend the legs slightly to curve them.

# Magical Mackerel

Mackerel swim in large schools near the surface of the sea. Their beautifully-patterned skin blends with the patterns of the sea to help them hide from predators.

Seabirds flying over the water, looking for a tasty meal, see only the darkness of the ocean. The mackerel has a dark wavy pattern on top which helps it blend with the deep water below.

Larger fish swimming up from the seabed see the brightness of the sunshine above and so the underside of the mackerel is a yellowish white color.

Follow the instructions on pages 4 and 5 to trace, cut out, and crease a paper fish pattern. Fold it into a 3-D model following the steps opposite. Decorate your fish and sharpen any creases between your fingernails.

**You will need**

Tracing paper and pencil
Stiff colored paper
Paper clips
Scissors and ruler
Knitting needle or old ballpoint pen
Craft knife (for adult use only)
Colored markers, pencil crayons, or crayons
Nylon thread and clear tape

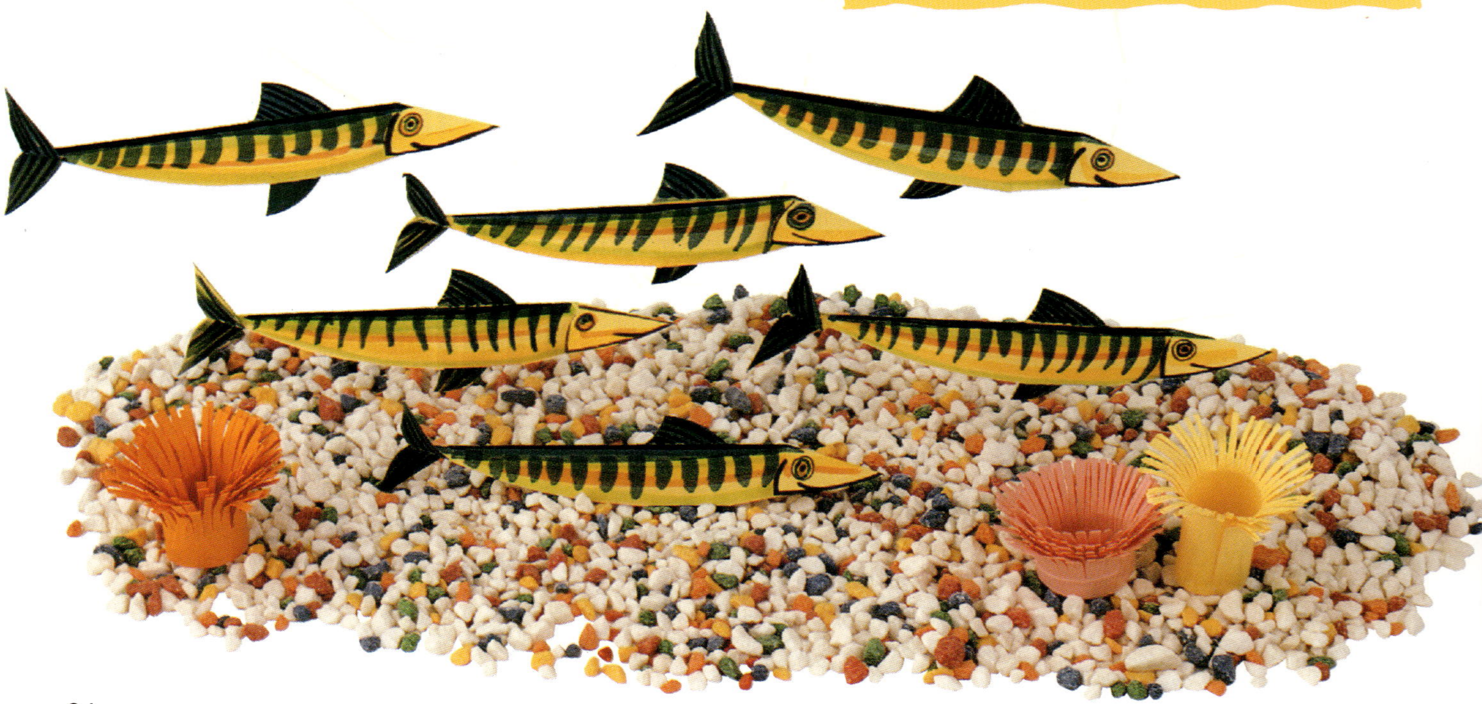

## FOLDING YOUR MACKEREL

1

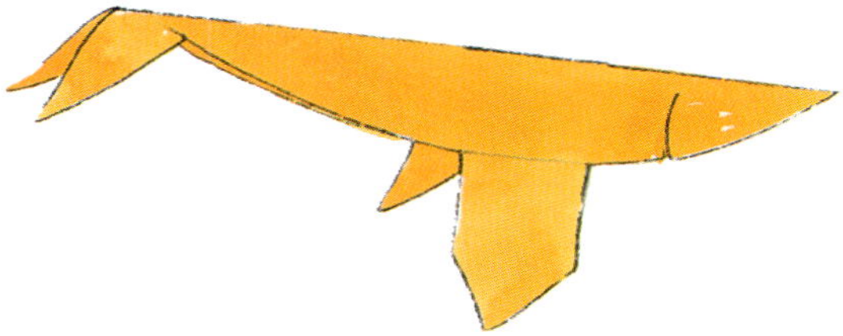

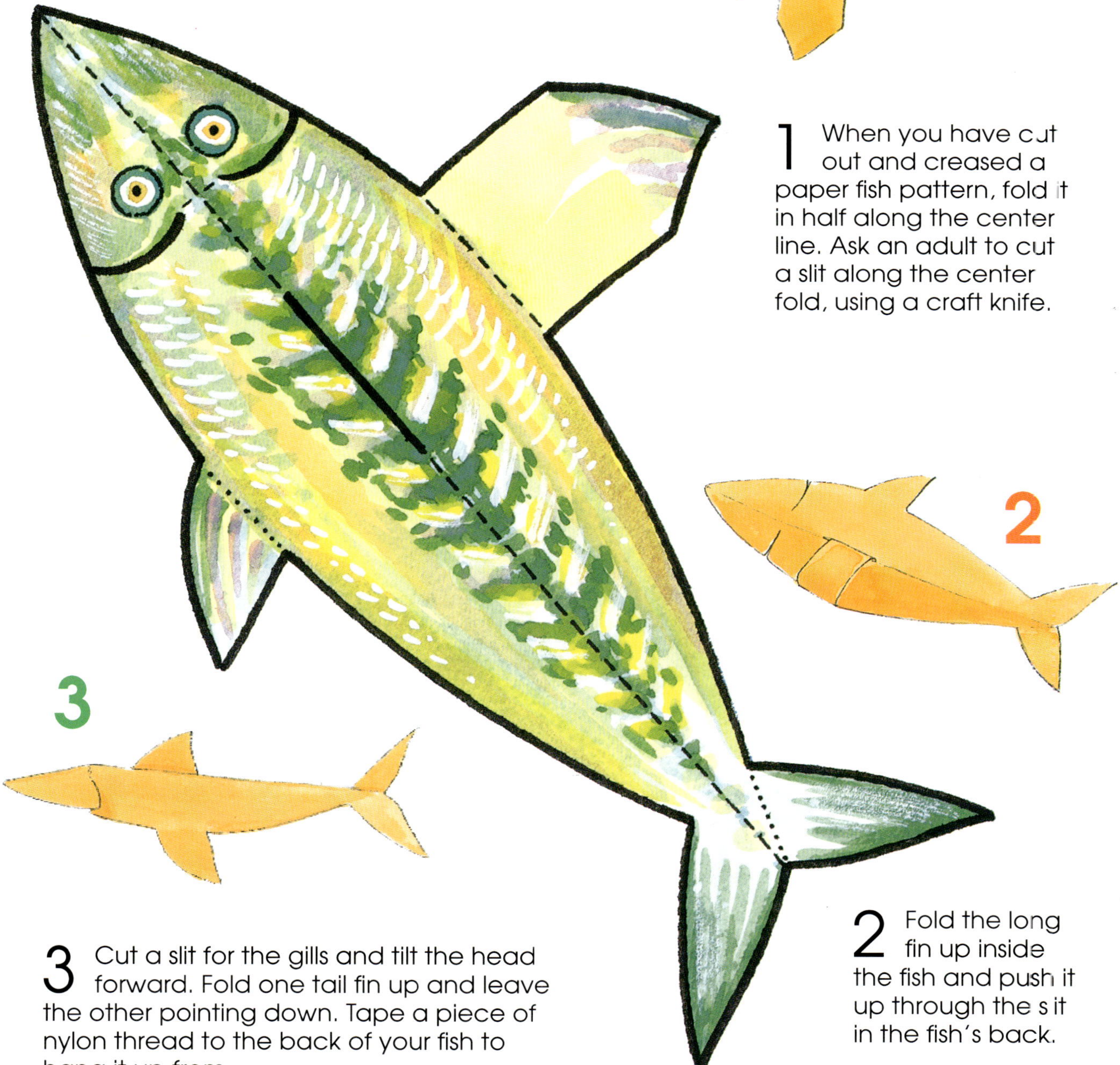

1 When you have cut out and creased a paper fish pattern, fold it in half along the center line. Ask an adult to cut a slit along the center fold, using a craft knife.

2

3

2 Fold the long fin up inside the fish and push it up through the slit in the fish's back.

3 Cut a slit for the gills and tilt the head forward. Fold one tail fin up and leave the other pointing down. Tape a piece of nylon thread to the back of your fish to hang it up from.

# Fearsome Sharks

Sharks are the most ferocious hunters in the ocean. When hunting, they are guided by their excellent sense of smell. They can detect traces of blood in the water over half a mile away.

Sharks never stop swimming because this movement keeps water, and the oxygen it carries, streaming through their gills. If they stopped, they would die of suffocation.

Follow the instructions on pages 4 and 5 to trace, cut out, and crease a paper shark pattern. Follow the steps opposite to fold your pattern into a 3-D model. Lay the shape flat again to decorate it and then refold your shark, sharpening any creases with your fingernails.

**You will need**

- Tracing paper and pencil
- Stiff colored paper
- Paper clips
- Scissors and ruler
- Knitting needle or ballpoint pen
- Craft knife (for adult use only)
- Colored markers, pencil crayons, or crayons

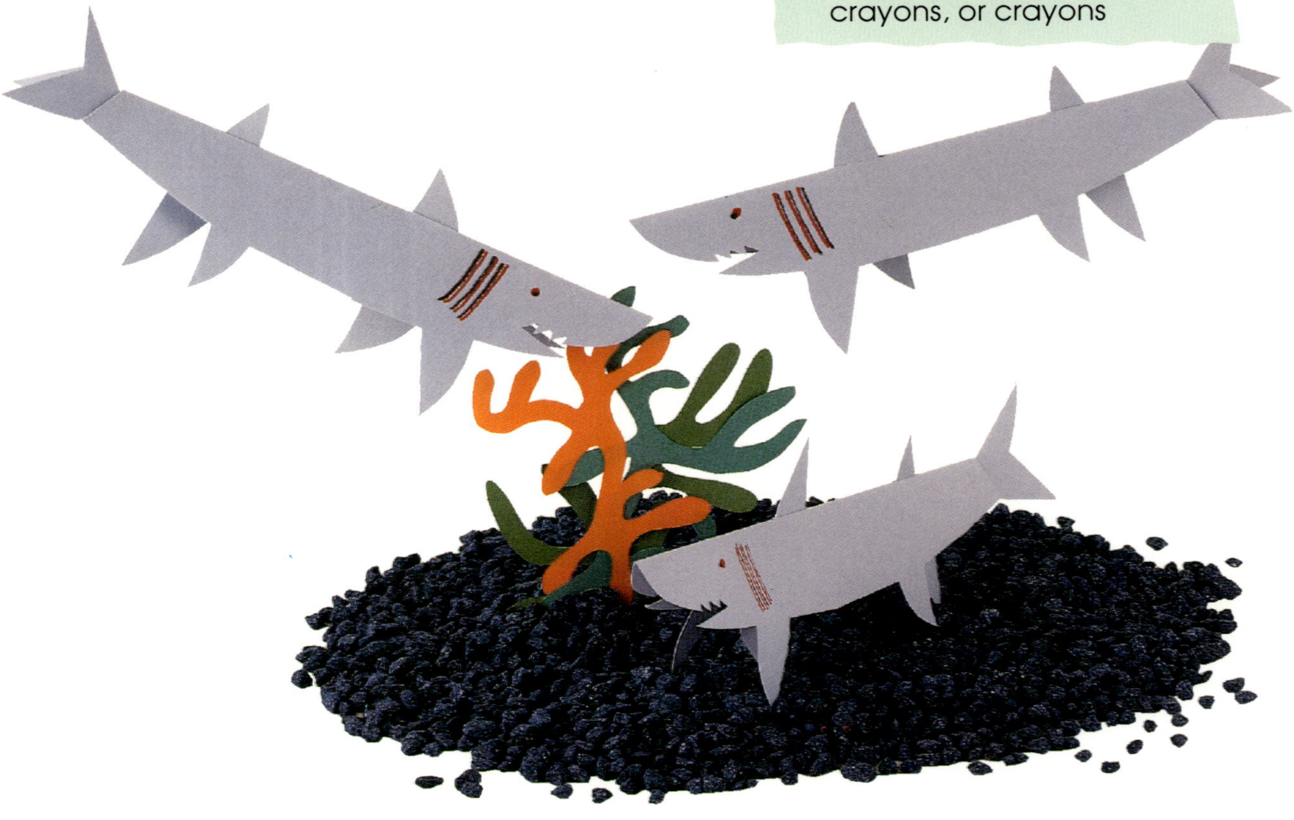

## FOLDING YOUR SHARK

1

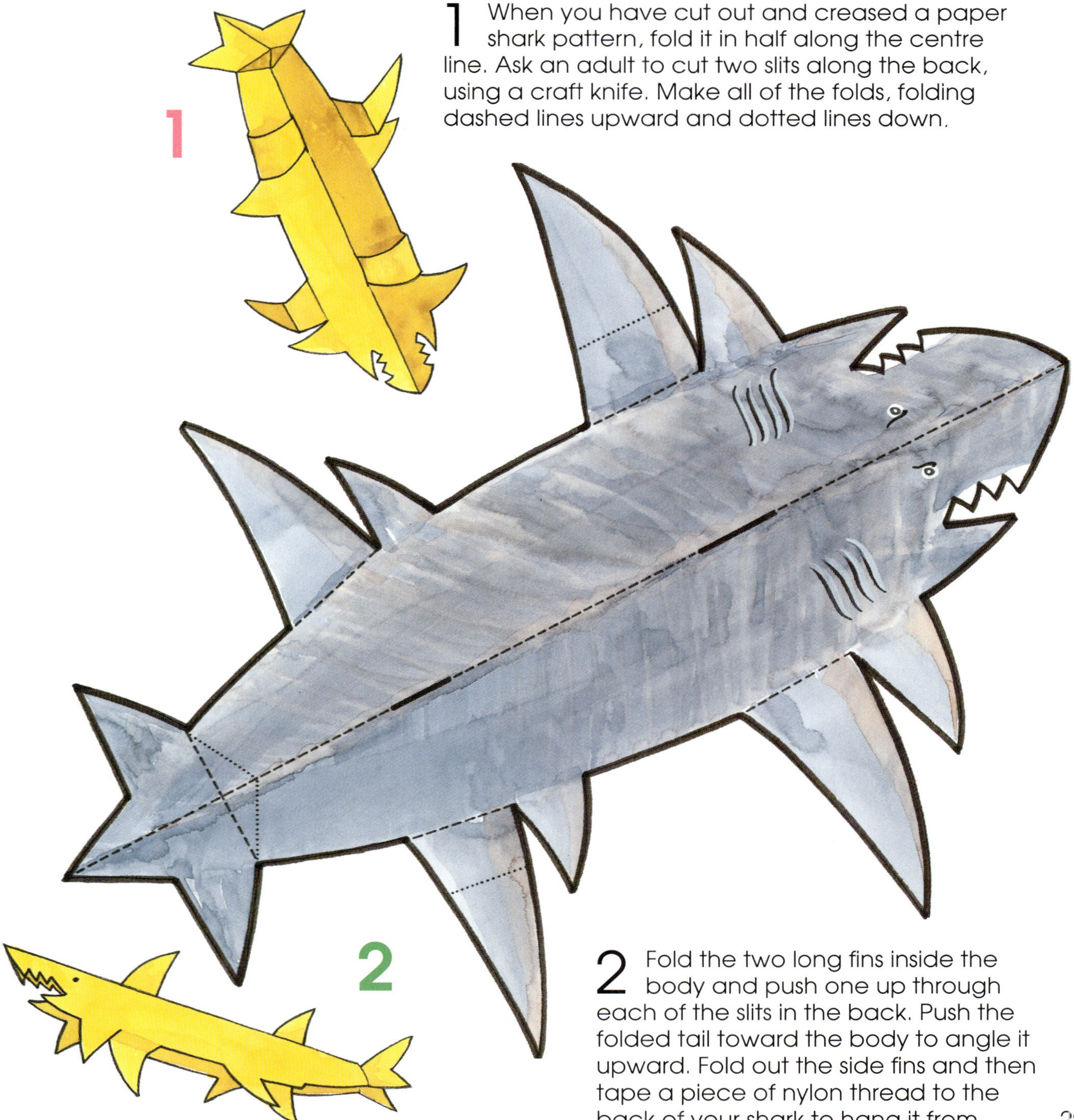

1 When you have cut out and creased a paper shark pattern, fold it in half along the centre line. Ask an adult to cut two slits along the back, using a craft knife. Make all of the folds, folding dashed lines upward and dotted lines down.

2

2 Fold the two long fins inside the body and push one up through each of the slits in the back. Push the folded tail toward the body to angle it upward. Fold out the side fins and then tape a piece of nylon thread to the back of your shark to hang it from.

# Graceful Green Sea Turtles

Turtles and their ancestors have lived on the Earth for about 250 million years and have changed very little over that time compared with other animals.

The green turtle lives in tropical seas where there are plenty of fish to eat, but at breeding time it crosses the Atlantic Ocean to Ascension Island. The female turtle lays about one hundred eggs in a pit in the sandy beach before returning to the sea. As soon as the baby turtles have hatched, instinct makes them dig their way out of the sand and head for the sea.

Follow the instructions on pages 4 and 5 to trace, cut out, and crease a paper turtle pattern. Then, follow the steps opposite to fold your pattern into a 3-D model. Lay it out flat to decorate it and then refold your model, sharpening the creases between your fingernails.

**You will need**

Tracing paper and pencil
Stiff colored paper
Paper clips
Scissors and ruler
Knitting needle or old ballpoint pen
Colored markers, pencil crayons, or crayons

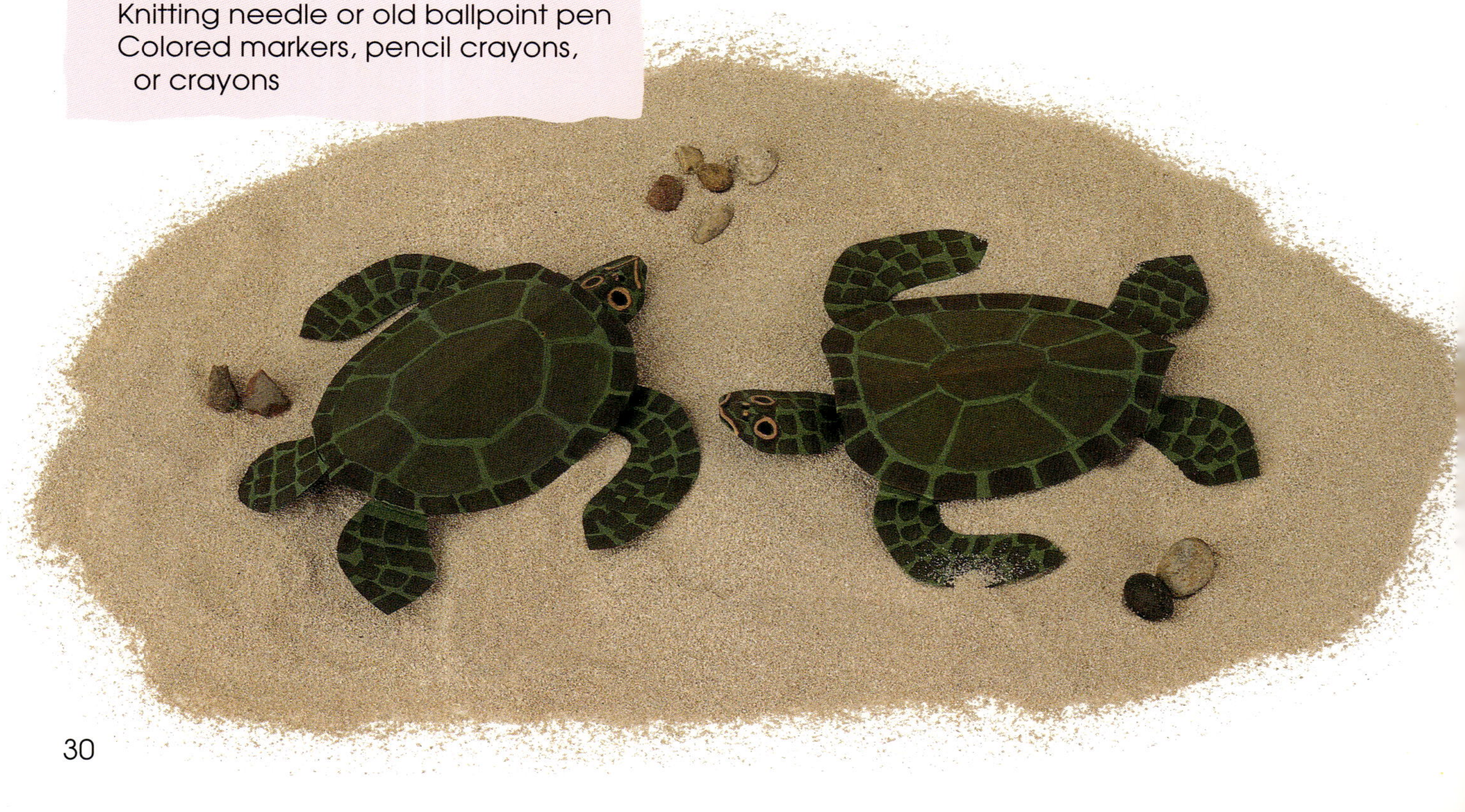

## FOLDING YOUR TURTLE

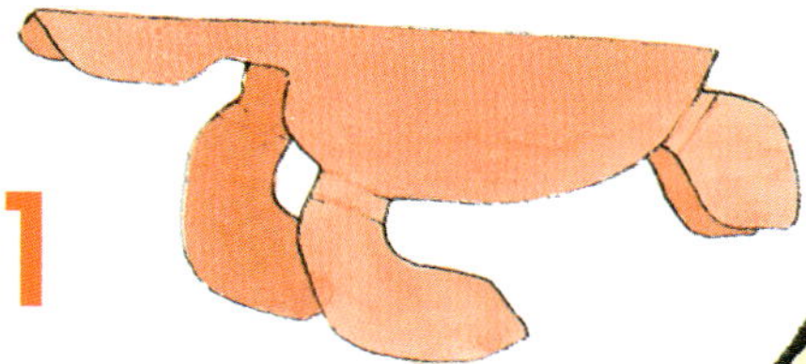

1

2 Make the inward folds on the flippers to tuck them under the shell.

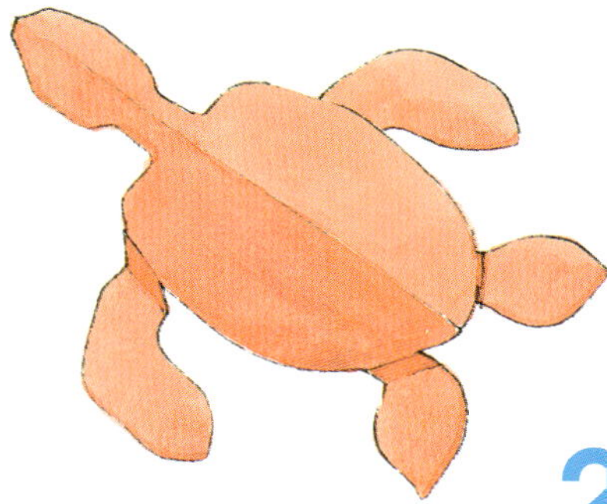

2

1 When you have cut out a paper turtle pattern and creased the fold lines, fold the turtle in half along the center line.

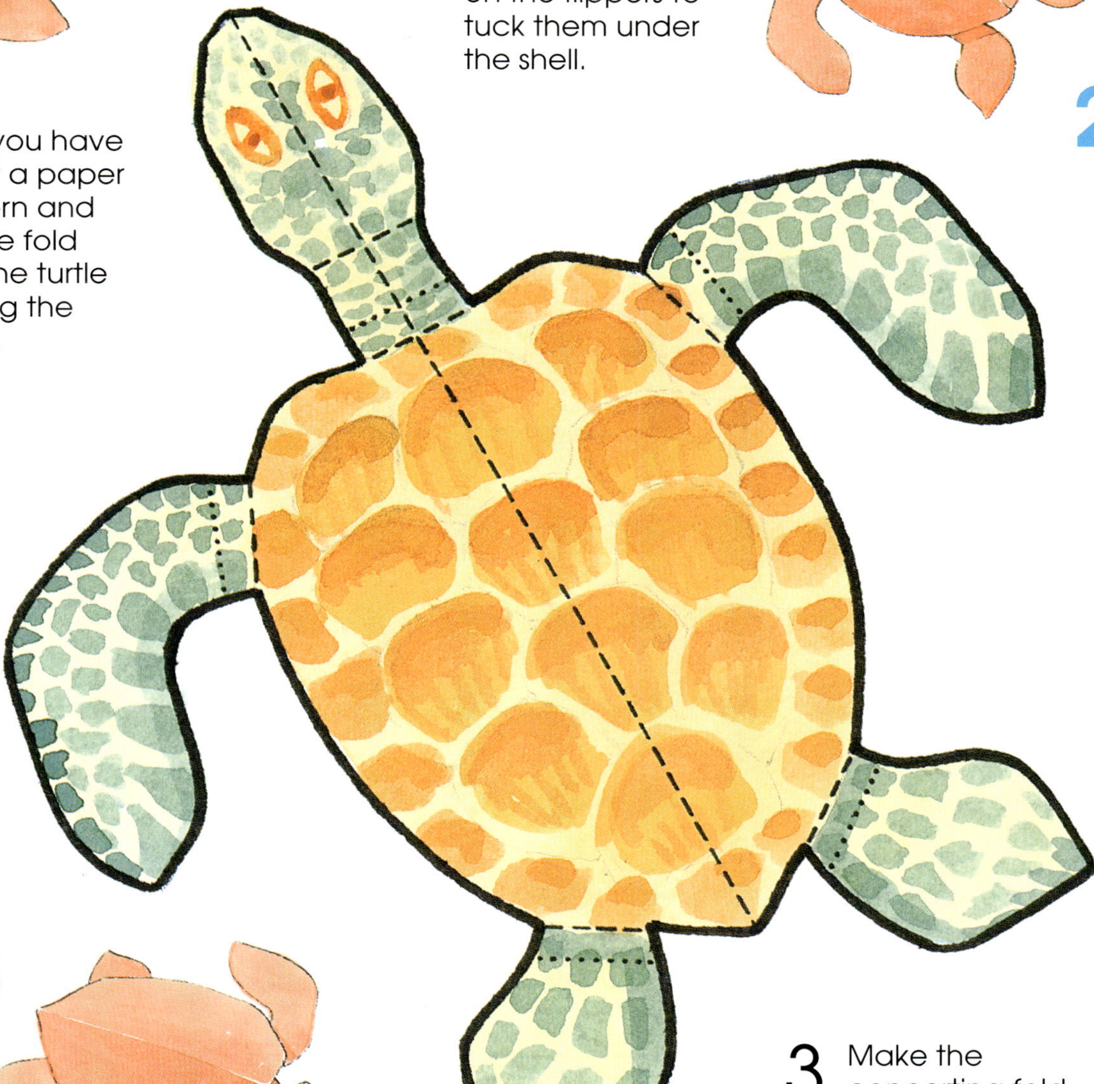

3

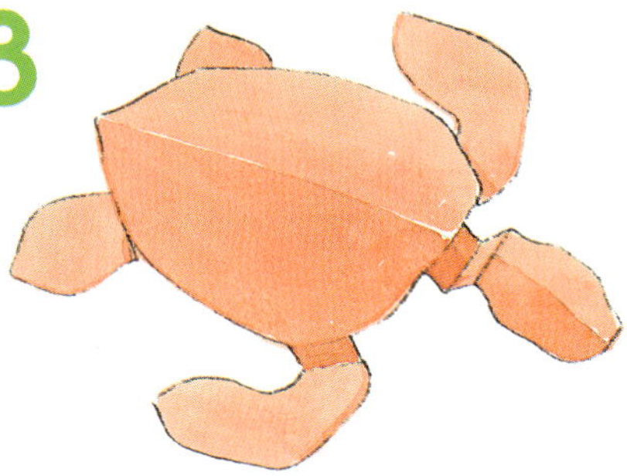

3 Make the concertina fold in the neck and push the head back toward the body. Curve the flippers.

# Questions and Answers

When you have made the sea creatures featured in this book test your knowledge by answering the questions in this quiz. All of the answers can be found in this book and they are printed at the bottom of the page for you to check your score.

**1. What do seals use to help them steer when they are swimming?**

**2. Are dolphins fish or mammals?**

**3. From how far away can a shark smell blood?**

**4. How long have sea turtles lived on Earth?**

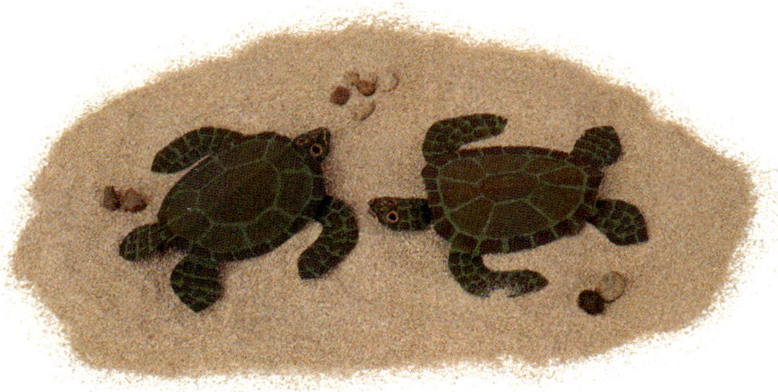

**5. What is unusual about a starfish's stomach?**

**6. How does an octopus move?**

**7. What color is a mackerel when seen from below?**

**8. What does a dolphin use to track its prey?**

**9. Which creature gives an electric shock?**

**10. How many arms does a starfish have?**

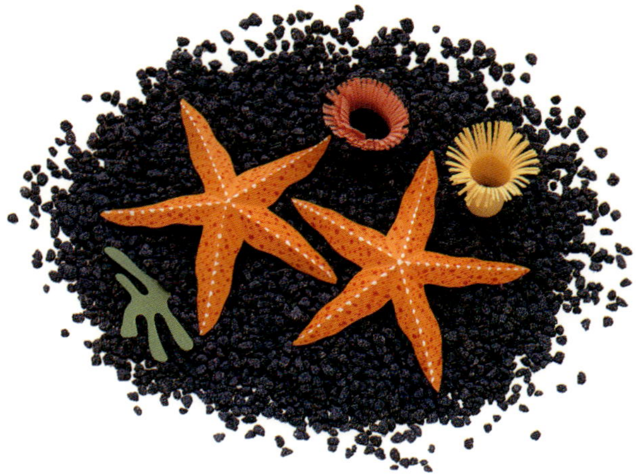

**11. How many different species of crab are there?**

**12. Which creature always lays its eggs on the same island?**

**13. Which garden pest is related to the octopus?**

**14. Why are coral reef fish so colorful?**

**15. In which part of the water do mackerel swim?**

## Answers

**1.** Their flippers. **2.** Mammals. **3.** Half a mile. **4.** 250 million years. **5.** It is outside its body. **6.** By sucking in water and jetting it out again. **7.** Yellowish white. **8.** Sonar or sound. **9.** The ray. **10.** Five. **11.** 4, 000. **12.** The green turtle. **13.** The slug. **14.** To blend with their surroundings. **15.** Near the surface.